Last of the Dons II

By Yolanda M. Lucero Tenorio

Antón Chico, New Mexico

This book is dedicated:

To **Don Salvador Tapia** y **los diez y seis** on our 200th Anniversary of the Anton Chico Land Grant 1822-2022. And to our ancestors that have stood up and protected the Anton Chico Land Grant.

Last of the Dons II

©2022 Yolanda M. Lucero Tenorio All Rights Reserved

ISBN: 979-8-218-11292-9

Cover photograph and design by Leroy Chris Tenorio.

Preface

In composing "Last of the Dons" a task of documenting and putting all the stories about our ancestors as told by the elders. Jim said, "the people of Anton Chico lived the real west"!

I will continue to record experiences of our grandfathers (the Dons) and grandmothers (the Doñas). This book will account for the travels along with documents.

The stories will continue to be told in conversational mode as would be over the kitchen table.

Contents:

La Mesita de los Ladrones:	1
Sandia Pueblo:	3
José Inés Tenorio:	7
Don Melaquias:	10
San José en Colonias:	18
Don Pedro Ulibarri:	20
Don José Guadalupe Gallegos:	21
"The Civil War Comes to New Mexico":	24
Don Antonio Bernabé Gallegos:	26
Don Fidel Gallegos:	27
Don Teodoro Madrid:	39
Upper Anton Chico:	45
Doña Dionicia Lucero Martínez:	49
Manuel Morales:	54
Doña Lola Sisneros:	60
St. Joseph's Catholic Church/Nuns:	66
Pat Garrett:	68
Antón Chico:	70
Don José Néstor García:	78
Don Zacarias y Terecita Salas:	81
Don Santos:	86
El Fileto:	89
Los Jaramillos:	91
George Jaramillo:	96
Don Florencio Aragón:	97

Don Fernando Baca:	101
Don Manuel Casaus:	107
Papá Luis Valverde:	109
Doña Tules:	110
Don Napoleón Campos:	114
Wilfred and Robert Hern:	118
Don Amadeo Tenorio Sr.:	120
Don Ruperto y Rosita Sandoval:	123
Miguel Gómez:	128
Duran and Salas:	129
Doña Martha Baca:	130
Esequiel C De Baca:	131
Don Rafael Lucero:	140
Doña Eulalia Leyba:	146
Don Andrés Lucero:	159
Don Juanito Lucero:	168
Don Rumaldo Lucero:	179
Don Demecio Lucero:	193
Doña Aurelia:	198
Don Pedro Lucero:	201
Don Merejildo Esquibel:	203
Don Leo Baca:	209
Don José Anastacio María Baca:	217
John Harrison:	221
Don Dionicio Castillo:	223
Don Demetrio Carrillo:	227
Don Cruz Lucero:	228

Mrs. Eva Aragón:	229
Miguel Gonzales:	232
Don Tomas Maestas:	234
Don Julián Maestas:	238
Don Onofre Márquez:	244
Don Silvestre Márquez:	250
Doña Manuelita Mink Nelson:	251
Don Nicasio Sánchez:	253
Kiko Gutiérrez:	255
Heraldo Mondragón and Alfonso Aragón:	256
Don Juan Bautista Olguin:	259
Don Timoteo Leyba:	262
Don Samuel Pino:	268
Don Esteban Romero:	271
Doña Tiburcia Olguin Castillo:	283
Don Felipe Romo:	285
Rick Romo:	285
Don Alejandro Bachicha:	288
Amigos:	289
Amigos de Maes:	292
Don José Domingo Maestas:	295
El Presidente:	306
Creencias/Querencias:	307
Dichos:	310
Acknowledgments:	317
Bibliography:	318

La Mesita de los Ladrones:

Source: La Mesita de los Ladrones.

La mesita de los Ladrones:

La cañada del Aguardiente and la mesita de Los Ladrones right above. The northwest of the Anton Chico Land Grant. In the mid 1930's taxes had to be paid and therefore the Board of Trustees mortgaged or sold the northwest corner of the Grant to Gross Kelly and Co. of Las Vegas, N.M. In Oct. 23, 1939, Gross Kelly sold the land to what was Farm Security Administration and now FHA at $58,751.10 for 26,464.46 acres of the Anton Chico Land Grant.

By Jan. 31, 1947, the FHA transferred and added the land to the Santa Fe National Forest and is called El Pueblo Area. [A story of Anton Chico Grant by Fidel S. Gallegos].

Los Sótanos:

At la mesita were sótanos [a hole with dirt that continues to sink down] useful to thieves. La Gavilla de Silva found the sótanos useful. Theft of livestock was evident since cattle hides had been dropped into the sótanos after all the cattle companies were causing a lot of problems with land grants.

Abuelo Don Juanito Lucero saw the sótanos and cattle hides that had been dropped in there. Pieces of lona [canvas] were also seen in the sótano.

En los Alamitos three or four miles north of Las Vegas was the home of Vicente Silva's wife. The questioning of her brother's death became too much of a burden for Vicente. Vicente also killed his wife because of her suspicious questioning and when the time came to bury her Vicente Silva too was killed by his own men and then buried him in the same embankment. His three men had lost the trust of Vicente Silva and feared for their life. [Pablo Lucero, personal communication].

Sandia Pueblo:

Figure: Our Lady of Sorrows Church [now El sanctuario de San Lorenzo]. Source of photo credit Abq. Museum. Photo taken circa 1880.

Tiwa Pueblos and the Hispano:

In 1540 the Spanish Explorer Francisco Coronado came to what is now Bernalillo and made his headquarters along the Rio Grande. The two Pueblos that were nearby were the Kuaua [Evergreen] and Tuf Shur Tia [Green Reed Place]. These were the two Tiwa Pueblos and became known as the Pueblo of Sandia. By Aug. 10, 1680, the Pueblo Revolt began. But the intermarriage of the Hispanos and the Natives from Sandia had strong ties.

The pueblo learned of the revolt and the residents of Bernalillo fled to "El Paso" known as "El Realito de San Lorenzo". For being spared they gave thanks to San Lorenzo and made a promesa.

Source: Los Matachines de Alcalde. Marie Markesteyn Photographer.

Los Matachines en Anton Chico:

Nuestra Señora de Dolores at Sandia Pueblo and the Matachines were part of the promesa in thanksgiving to San Lorenzo.

The danza an influence that the Spanish brought from Spain and Los Matachines celebrated and danced in Anton Chico for some years. [Father Stanley, THE ANTONCHICO (New Mexico) STORY, 1975].

A celebration at Our Lady of Sorrows at Sandia Pueblo is still celebrated today with a procession that begins from a private home and to church for a mass. The dance that the Matachines perform includes the young girls dressed in white and their purity.

The dancers wear headdresses called "cupiles". The mask worn is an image of a saint that they pick. A "wooden trident" is called a Palma representing the "Trinity" which stands as a shield.

The whole dance is in concept of a battle of good and evil. The soldiers serve as shields and the guaje as the sword.

Teresa Tenorio Lives at Sandia Pueblo:

Teresa Tenorio and her family were a part of Sandia Pueblo. Maria Teresa Bonifacia Tenorio was born in 1827 and baptized at Nuestra Señora de Dolores at Sandia Pueblo. Teresa spent about 20 years at Sandia Pueblo with her father Francisco Tenorio, Mother Rita Gurule, brothers Juan Bautista born in 1823 and Jose Abran born in 1840.

The family was familiar or a part of the Matachines danzas during the holidays and church celebration at Nuestra Señora de Dolores at Sandia Pueblo.

Jose Manuel Tenorio:

Maria Teresa's grandfather Jose Manuel Tenorio was born in 1775 and married María Antonia Ramírez in 1796 in Santa Fe.

Jose Manuel Tenorio and Maria Antonia Ramirez had 15-children, Francisco being the oldest, Antonio Tenorio also a son, Juana Maria, and Maria Casilda. Between 1797 and 1802 three of six children were born in Santa Fe. Ygnacia Marta Baptized at San Miguel del Bado 1804. [Nostrand L. Richard. El Cerrito, New Mexico, 2003].

Juan Bautista, Juana Nepomucena, Claonica, Maria De La Cruz, Abran, Ignacio, Julian, Juan P., and Maria Teresa Bonifacia appear on the 1850 Census of La Cuesta, San Miguel, N.M. Territory.

El Cerrito:

Jose Manuel Tenorio was an original Cerrito grantee petitioner on March 6, 1824. He was buried in 1836 at El Cerrito. Jose Eduardo, the son of Jose Manuel Tenorio and Maria Antonia Ramirez was the first burial on November 26, 1827, at El Cerrito and was probably buried at La Cuesta. Father Juan Caballero was the priest at San Miguel del Vado 1825-1829.

By the time Maria Teresa B. was around 20 years old. Francisco and Rita, her parents made the journey on horse and wagon to San Miguel del Vado and to El Cerrito. By 1847 Maria De La Cruz Tenorio was born and Christened at San Miguel del Vado. [Nostrand L. Richard. El Cerrito, New Mexico, 2003].

Anton Chico:

The next journey was made to Anton Chico by Teresa, her mother Rita, brother Abran, and sister Cruz according to census records. Abuelita Teresa was now 36 years old and single. Her travels were horse and wagon. We know that many dangers such as distance to their destination, wildlife, and hostile encounters were treacherous.

By Jan. 25, 1863, Jose Ines Tenorio was born to Maria Teresa Tenorio and Christened at Saint Joseph Catholic Church, Anton Chico, New Mexico. Abuelo Jose Ines Tenorio was of light complexion and had light brown hair. [Altagracia Tenorio Urioste, personal communication, Nov. 5, 2018].

Padrinos for Jose Ines were Domingo Pacheco his uncle and Cruz Tenorio Pacheco his aunt. The Census of 1870 shows that they lived in Tecolotito with Rita Gurule, her mother, and her brother Jose Abran Tenorio.

Maria Teresa may have been one of the first to light a fire in the village of Tecolotito. [Altagracia Tenorio Urioste, personal communication, Nov. 5, 2018].

Another family that lived at Sandia Pueblo was Juan Bautista Jaramillo born [1794-1/3/1873] and married 2/13/1815 at Sandia to Maria Ursula Montoya born 1800-1/13/1875.

Jose Ines Tenorio:

Jose Ines Tenorio 1863–

Name Jose Ines Tenorio
Given names Jose Ines
Surname Tenorio

Facts and events | Families | Notes | Interactive tree

before April 22, 1863
Anton Chico, Guadalupe, New Mexico, USA

Note: Padrinos: Domingo Pacheco and Cruz Tenorio (Cruz was the sister of the child's mother) They were from Tecolotito

Source: www.hgrcnm.orgwebtrees/individual.

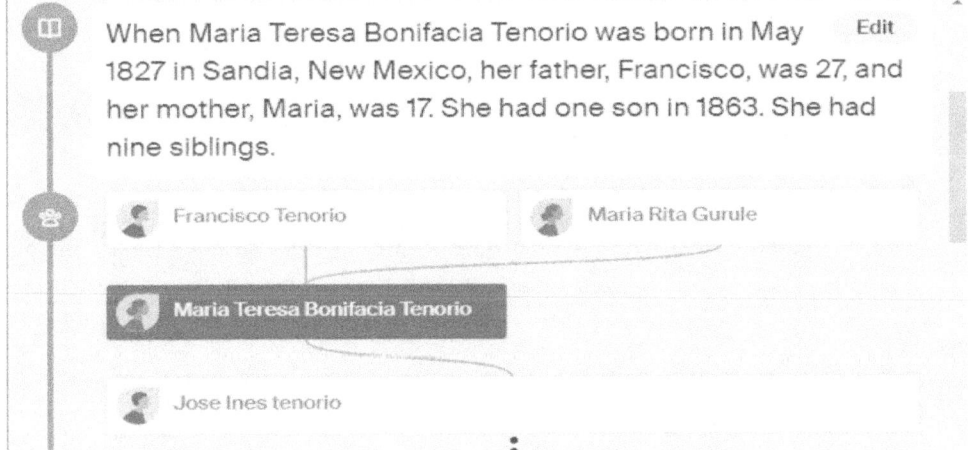

When Maria Teresa Bonifacia Tenorio was born in May 1827 in Sandia, New Mexico, her father, Francisco, was 27, and her mother, Maria, was 17. She had one son in 1863. She had nine siblings.

Francisco Tenorio | Maria Rita Gurule

Maria Teresa Bonifacia Tenorio

Jose Ines tenorio

1840 Birth of brother

Her brother Abran was born in March 1840 in Sandia, New Mexico, when Maria Teresa Bonifacia was 12 years old.

Abran Tenorio
1840–

March 1840 • Sandia pueblo, Sandoval County, New Mexico, USA

1843 Birth of brother

Her brother Juan P. was born in 1843 when Maria Teresa Bonifacia was 16 years old.

Juan P. Tenorio
1843–

1843

1844 Birth of brother

Her brother Julian was born in 1844 when Maria Teresa Bonifacia was 17 years old.

Julian Tenorio
1844–

1844

1847 Birth of sister

Her sister Maria De La Cruz was born in September 1847 in San Miguel, New Mexico, when Maria Teresa Bonifacia was 20 years old.

Maria De La Cruz Tenorio
1847–

Sep 1847 • San Miguel, New Mexico

1848 Birth of sister

Her sister Claonica was born in 1848 when Maria Teresa Bonifacia was 21 years old.

Claonica Tenorio
1848–

1848

1863 Birth of son

Her son Jose Ines was born on January 25, 1863, in Tecolotito, New Mexico.

Jose Ines tenorio
1863–

25 Jan 1863 • Tecolotito, San Miguel, New Mexico, USA

Source: Ancestry Family Tree Maria Teresa Tenorio.

Cerrito Bernal:

No.	Surname	Given Name(s)	Sex	Age	Occupation	Real Estate Value ($)	Agriculture Schedule	Comments
		Table A.2. Population in El Cerrito, October 1850 (continued)						
31	Sandoval	Petrita	F	30				
		Prudencia	F	5				
		José	M	1				
32	Sinaco	Antonio	M	28	laborer	50		
		Asención	F	25				
		Ramón	M	12				
33	Tenorio	Francisco	M	50	laborer	50		Francisco, probably the oldest son of José Manuel (1824: 1 of 15); mar to Dolores Mondragón in 1816 (27: 267)
		María Rita	F	40				
		María Teresa	F	20				
		Juan P.	M	7				
		Julián	M	6				
		Ignacio	M	12				
		Abrán	M	5				
		María de la Cruz	F	4				
		Claonica	F	3				
34	Tenorio	Luis	M	76				
		María Antonia	F	38				
		Total: 130 people						

SOURCE: U.S. Bureau of the Census, Population Schedules of the Seventh Census [1850], roll 469, pp. 57–60 (29A, 29B, 30A, 30B).

NOTES: Assistant Marshal James D. Robinson took the census in San Miguel County between 12 October and 20 November 1850. He listed all people under four place headings: Las Vegas, La Cuesta, San Miguel, and Tuckelata (Tecolote). Robinson was in El Cerrito, found within "La Cuesta," on 19–20 October. All people on pages 57–60, which contained the El Cerrito families, were born in New Mexico Territory. No information was recorded under "Color," except for the two people in household #20 who Robinson noted as "Ind" (Indian). Robinson was apparently the twenty-five-year-old Pennsylvania-born barber whose name was given in Santa Fe as David Robinson (1850, roll 468:693). An Anglo, his knowledge of written Spanish was imperfect, he neglected to give the villages he enumerated, and in the four pages containing El Cerrito families, he repeated six families. His count for El Cerrito in 1850 is not altogether accurate. In this table abbreviations given in the census are written out, spelling is systematized, and accents are added. Ages are given as reported in census; complete names if known are noted in brackets.

Source: Richard L. Nostrand, EL CERRITO, NEW MEXICO EIGHT GENERATIONS IN A SPANISH VILLAGE, p. 186.

El Huerfano:

The Cerrito along highway 84 on the Tecolotito turn off to 386 and to Tecolotito.

Don Melaquias:

Melaquias watched the evening news at Juliana's [sister] and Telesfor's [brother in-law's] house. Don Felipe, Melaquia's brother, also came along with the grandsons to watch television. Every afternoon they all gathered and watched the only black and white TV available to the family.

The evening TV schedule consisted of black and white Westerns with Roy Rogers or Gene Autry. Only four local channels broadcasted from Albuquerque. The family watched television until the 10:00 P.M. news ended.

Melaquias understood the English language and he often interpreted the news or even the weather report to his family. The news report on one occasion was interpreted by Melaquias to his brother Felipe and brother in-law Telesfor. The news cast event was nothing like the interpretation given by Tio Melaquias and he said, "Que le habían tirado con tomates al rey de Méjico". Melaquias's nephews immediately told Melaquias, "no dijo eso". Melaquias said, "Ustedes no saben nada".

When the weatherman reported that there was a possibility of showers and breezes. His brother-in-law Telesfor and Felipe asked him about the weather. The weather interpreted by Melaquias was, "Aires esta tarde y posible showeres".

Juan:

Figure: Left to Right. Three men unidentified, Juan Tenorio Sr. Courtesy Mary Alice Villanueva Chavez.

The Atarque:

Mamá Amada often sent Juan to the atarque for lunch delivery. Don Felipe and the men were working on the Tecolotito dam a sponsored job with WPA. Amada prepared lunch for Don Felipe and Juan walked during lunch to deliver the lunch bucket for his father. Everything was packed in a 4 lb. Manteca [lard] bucket the lunch pail that was used by most of the men. No ants or unwanted pests could get into the bucket. 2 boiled eggs, 2 boiled potatoes, homemade bread, salt, and pepper were all packed in the Manteca bucket.

Figure: Atarque [dam] Tecolotito in the Pecos River. Courtesy Ray Lucero

A Day's Work for WPA:

A lot of sandstone was taken from the land grant and cut into blocks of approximately 8- and 10-inches wide x 16 to 24 inches long. The men used hand tools such as chisels and hammers for the rock work to shape the many blocks for the two dams the Tecolotito and the dam for the Dilia ditch. A lot of stone was needed for the country schools also. The horse and wagon were the source for hauling the stone and the heavy work.

Arroyos were also covered with branches for the prevention of erosion through the WPA projects.

Some of the men worked hard on the projects but then some men played cards or rolled dice in the arroyos all day long.

[Manuel Lucero, personal communication]

The Bull:

Juan had been having trouble with a bull getting into his alfalfa field. His nephew Joe was usually available to chase out the bull but of course there had to be payment.

Juan was getting ready to go to Anton Chico and saw the bull in the alfalfa field again. Juan called Joe and told him to take out the bull and he would pay him a quarter. Joe ran down to the field and chased out the bull.

Joe quickly went to see if his aunt Louisa had his cuara [quarter]. Louisa said, "que cuara, ni cuara" ya tu tío Juan está cansado de pagarles por todo". Joe ran back to the field and opened the gate and put the bull back into the pasture.

When Tío Juan got home he saw that the bull was still at the pasture. Juan asked, Louisa, ¿que este cabron del Joe no saco el toro?" She said, "no se, El andaba buscando un cuara".

Tío Juan called Joe again and asked him about the bull. And Joe told him that he didn't get paid, so he put the bull back into the pasture. Tío Juan promised him two cuaras to take out the bull again.

El Glue:

Luciano Salas was a shoe repair man in Anton Chico. He had the best military type of glue for his shoe repair business. A bucket full! Juan Tenorio and Nick Hern knew of the glue and how well it worked on the automobile and tractor tubes. Cutting a piece of tube and putting a bit of glue was like a two-way patch. Flat tires and bad tires were always a problem for the men but to get glue from Luciano was no easy task.

Luciano easily became annoyed with Nick Hern and Juan Tenorio telling them, "Cada ratito vienen a chingar por mi glue". "y yo lo necesito para mi negocio". Nick only needed a tiny little jar of glue and they finally managed to get some glue along with an ass chewing.

The Wrecking Yard:

Luciano Salas also had a wrecking yard and sold car parts. This time Andalecio Romero and Juan Tenorio needed a lift spring and Luciano quoted the men $2.50 for the spring. Luciano got under the car and came back out where the men were at and said, "cincuenta centavos y si la quitas tu". Andalecio got under the car and took off the spring.

Marijuana:

Luciano Salas had many ongoing projects another project was planting marijuana. This time the illegal

plants were reported to the officials. Luciano lied to the cops sending them to another residence and they went on a wild goose chase.

In the meantime, he pulled out the marijuana plants and threw them over to the neighbor's place.

Figure Left to right Altagracia Tenorio Urioste, Felipe Tenorio Courtesy Altagracia Tenorio Urioste.

Figure: Altagracia Tenorio Urioste, Cheerleader with Anton Chico Tigers in 1962. Courtesy Altagracia Tenorio Urioste.

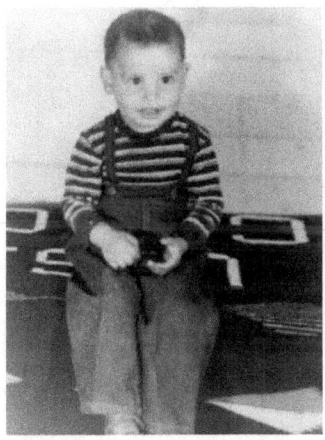

Figure: Louis Manuel Tenorio. Courtesy Eileen Tenorio.

Figure: Left to right. Gilberto Tenorio *[standing]*, Maximiliano Tenorio *[sitting on truck]*, Teresa Carrillo *[sitting on truck]*, Ermelindo Carrillo. *Courtesy Betty Tenorio Goins.*

Figure: Left to right. Ermelindo Carrillo, Teresa Carrillo, Gilberto Tenorio, [front kneeling] Maximiliano Tenorio. Courtesy Betty Tenorio Goins.

Prestedonia [Nona]:

Figure: Prestedonia [Nona] Baca Lucero. Courtesy Ben Lucero.

Prestedonia was the daughter of Rosa Tenorio and Lorenzo Baca. Rosa had three sisters Teresita, Juliana, Serafica, and two brothers Felipe and Melaquias Tenorio.

San José en Colonias:

Figure: San José en Colonias. Courtesy Stefanie Joann Gallegos.

The beginning of the colonies in the 1700's and San Jose en Colonias began with a small adobe building. Then in the 1820's the second section was constructed. The third part of the church its largest is when the three towers were erected. During this time Colonias was at its busiest and highest population.

Plantations, ranches, and communities were established in the 1780's. The villagers farmed and were sheepherders. They hunted buffalo in the fall. From 1930 to 1940 the village population was around 850. [www.coloniasnm.com/html]

Figure: Left to Right. Back Row. Valentin Ulibarri, Unidentified, Middle Row. Unidentified, Unidentified, Pedro, Front Row. Unidentified, Ramoncita Ulibarri Maestas, Clara Baca Ulibarri [wife], unidentified, Francisquita Ulibarri. Courtesy Myria Trini Mandel.

Jose baptized 3/27/1869, Fulgencia baptized 2/8/1871, Jose Basilio baptized 4/21/1873, Maria Estefana baptized 3/1/1876, Francisca married 8/20/1899, Cleotilde baptized 6/6/1883, Pedro Antonio baptized 6/4/1886, Valentin baptized 12/23/1888, Maria Ramona baptized 11/11/1891. [Sacramental Records from the Archives of the Archdiocese of Santa Fe, N. Mex. Baptisms Antón Chico La Yglesia de San José 1857-1897]. [Sacramental Records from the Archives of the Archdiocese of Santa Fe, N. Mex. Marriages Antón Chico La Yglesia de San José April 1857-December 1940].

Valentín Ulibarri was the owner of el negro cowboy. The cowboy that helped the women when the men went to herd sheep. El negro cowboy helped with bringing wood or work that might be too hard for women. [Reymundo Maestas, personal communication].

Don Pedro Ulibarri:

Figure: Left to right. Tio Pedro Ulibarri, and sister Francisquita Ulibarri "Cuca", [and Great Grandmother of Myria] Courtesy. Myria Trini Mandrel.

Pedro Great Grand uncle was bucked off a horse and got a compound fracture in his thigh near the hip. Pedro pulled the piece of bone out of his leg and buried it as his mother Clara Baca Ulibarri told him to do so. Perhaps due to a querencia [belief] that his mother believed in.

Pedro's Creativity:

Tío Pedro enjoyed making toys for the children. He made tops with thread spools for the boys and for the girls Pedro made doll furniture out of copper wire.

Pedro made whips using a stick and leather. He also made his own frame to weave rugs. Making hot pads and potholders was something he enjoyed creating with his hands. [Myria Trini Mandrel, personal communication, Oct. 8, 2020].

Don José Guadalupe Gallegos:

Figure: Jose Guadalupe Gallegos. Courtesy Stefanie Joann Gallegos.

Abril 13 de 1828. Bautize a Jose Guadalupe Gallegos, de 2 dias de nacido, de San Jose, hijo legitimo de Jose Fernando Gallego y de Juliana Padilla. Abuelos Paterno's: Toribio Gallego y Bernarda Baca. Abuelos Maternos: Diego Padilla y Nicolasa Lopez. Padrinos: Thomas Baca y Micaela Ulibarri.

Source: Hispanic Genealogical Research Center of New Mexico, Baptisms San Miguel del Vado Pecos Mission 1799-1829. P. 52

Family:

Jose Guadalupe Gallegos was born 4/13/1828 to 5/18/1867. He married 15-year-old Josefa Gutierres at San Miguel del Vado by Father Jose Francisco Leyba.

The 1860 census recorded 4 children Ladislado, Bernabe, Maria Viviana, and Juan de Dios. By 1870 San Jose en Colonias indicate 2 more children, Silviano and Guadalupe.

Civil War Service [1854, 1861-1862]:

Jose Guadalupe a native New Mexican was a Military leader in 1854 whom served as a Brigadier General in the volunteer Mounted Militia of New Mexico territory. They protected the communities against Native attacks.

Before the Battle of Glorieta Pass, Guadalupe was a Union field and staff Colonel in the Civil War. He served as a commander of the 3rd N. Mex. volunteer infantry and commander of the Hatch's Ranch military post.

Politics:

Jose Guadalupe represented the county of San Miguel in 4 of the 6 assemblies of the Territory Legislature between 1855-1861: serving as House Speaker, and Council President. Jose was one of the founding members of the Historical Society of N. Mex.

Rancher:

Jose Guadalupe was a rancher and met his fate while crossing the Pecos River on his buckboard 5/18/1867.

Source: Jose Guadalupe Gallegos, Wikipedia.org.

Source: Jose Guadalupe Buckboard. Courtesy Stefanie Joann Gallegos.

Compact tree of Jose Guadalupe Gallegos

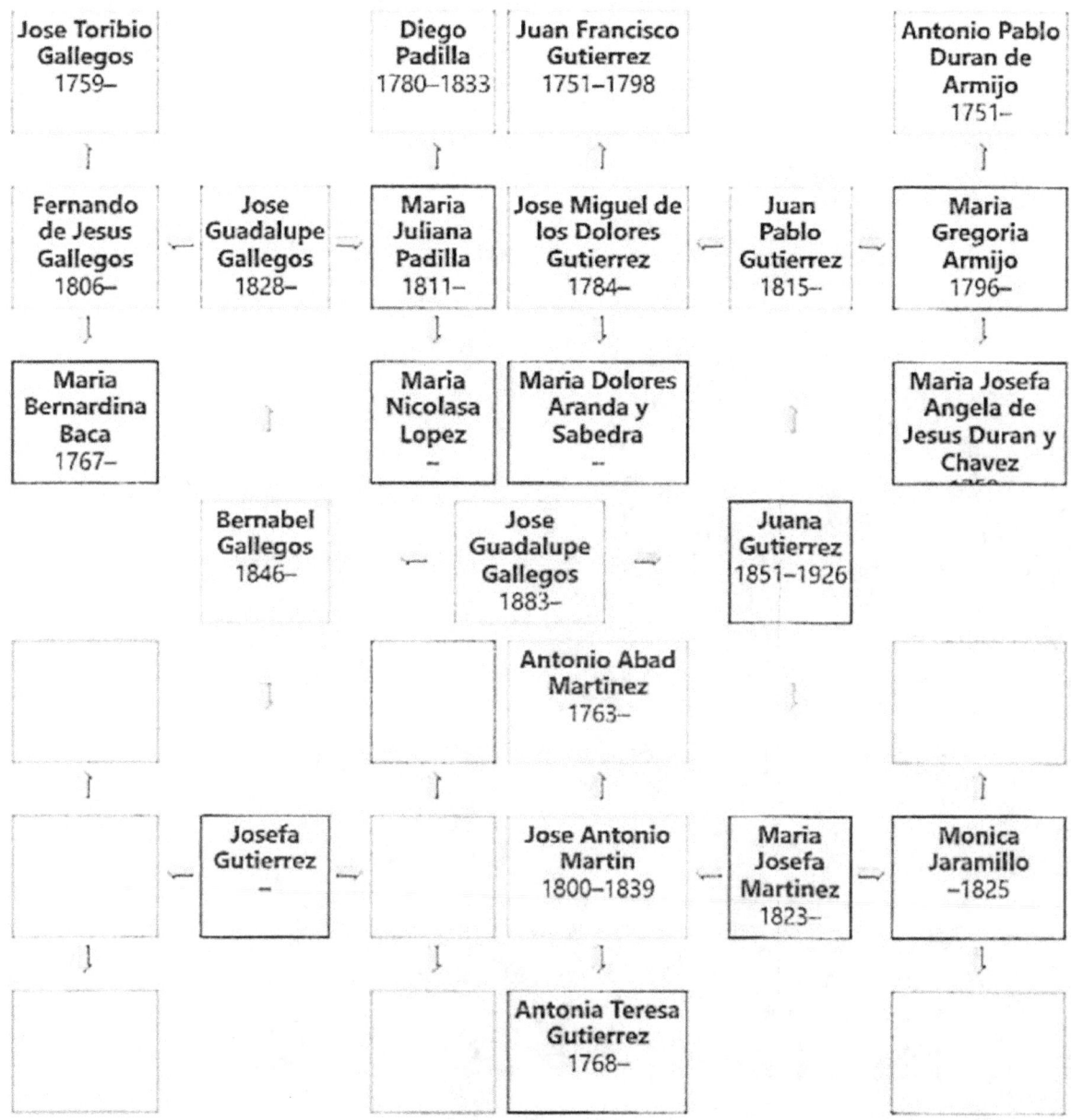

Source: Hispanic Genealogy Ctr. of New Mexico.

"The Civil War Comes to New Mexico":

Figure: Colonel Jose Guadalupe Gallegos of Colonias. Courtesy of Stefanie Joann Gallegos.

by Fidel S. Gallegos

The Civil War had come to New Mexico! Colonel Jose Guadalupe Gallegos, my great grandfather, was already in the Union Army with the First Regiment when Governor Henry Connelley issued a Proclamation dated September 9, 1861, calling for volunteers. The volunteers were to resist an invasion by armed forces from the state of Texas.

On August 26, 1861, Jose Guadalupe Gallegos of Colonias was commissioned a Field and Staff Colonel with the First Regiment, New Mexico Volunteers, in the Army of the United States. On September 27, 1861, Colonel Gallegos was transferred to the Third Regiment and Colonel Christopher Carson, known as Kit Carson, took commend of the First Regiment.

During the Civil War in New Mexico, there were five regiments with their respective commanding officers as follows: First Regiment, Colonel Christopher Carson; Second Regiment, Colonel Miguel Pino; Third Regiment, Colonel Jose Guadalupe Gallegos; Fourth Regiment, Colonel Gabriel R. Paul; Fifth Regiment, Colonel B. S. Roberts.

In February, 1862, General Henry H. Sibley, leading the Confederate forces, marched northward with an army of 2,600 men for the main conflict in New Mexico. Actually, General Sibley was General Canby;s brother-in-law. Edward R. S. Canby, commanding the Union Forces, was a colonel during the Battle of Valverde, but his troops called him "general" even though he was not a brigadier general until July of 1862. The Civil War Battle of Valverde occurred the morning of February 21, 1862, 29 miles south of the town of Socorro, New Mexico. General Canby (with about 3,800 men) met General Sibley and his men at the Valverde river crossing. It was here that the battle took place.

At the time of the battle, the Third Regiment was temporarily under the command of Lieutenant Colonel Jose Maria Valdez. Colonel Jose Guadalupe Gallegos did not take part in this battle. He was retained at Fort Union with some Union troops as a precaution against a possible Confederate invasion from the southeast. Jose Guadalupe Gallegos was a brigadier general with the Mounted Militia of New Mexico during the Apache Campaign. He had an encounter with the Jicarilla and Mescalero Apaches on July 3, 1854, at the Junction of the Rivers Mora and Sapello. Many Apaches were killed. Since Colonel Gallegos had battle experience, and being the only officer of high rank in Fort Union at the time, perhaps, General Canby figured that he was capable of defending Fort Union. He was in charge of the Federal troops that were left there to guard the fort.

The battle of Valverde lasted all day. The Confederates were victorious. The First and the Third New Mexico Regiments suffered heavy casualties. There were 100 Union soldiers dead and 122 wounded as compared to Confederate casualties of 36 men dead and 150 wounded. Captain Rafael Chacon, who was with the First Regiment, wrote the following in his diary:

"About four or five o'clock in the afternoon, the bulk of the enemy cavalry addressed themselves to delivering an attack on the positions occupied by my regiment and that of Colonel Gallegos', which was temporarily under the command of Colonel Valdez. The field was covered with blood, horses, torn and dismembered limbs, and heads separated from their bodies--a spectacle that was horrible."

After the Battle of Valverde, the Confederate objective was Fort Union, northwest of Colonias, a storehouse of ammunition and supplies. The Texans had stormed thier way through Valverde, Socorro, Belen, Peralta, Albuquerque and Santa Fe, moving ever northward.

Colonel John P. Slough came south to New Mexico with six companies of Colorado Volunteers to aid in the defense of Fort Union. The Colorado Volunteers, as well as New Mexico Volunteers and Federal troops, engaged the Rebels at Glorieta and Apache Canyon blocking the way to Fort Union. Lieutenant Colonel Manuel Chavez, who was with the Second Regiment under Colonel Miguel Pino, is credited with guiding Major John M. Chivington to the Texan's wagons that were burned at Johnson's Ranch near Glorieta Pass. Burning the wagons proved decisive as the Confederates lost their supplies. Major Chivington was a member of the Colorado Volunteers.

The Battle of Apache Canyon lasted only about three hours, but the fighting was furious while it lasted. The statements on Confederate losses in dead, wounded and captured vary from 131 to 223. The total Union casualties have been placed between 21 and 29..

An undated message contained in the Army service record of Colonel Gallegos, was sent by an unknown captain to Lieutenant Colonel William J. L. Nicodemus who was with the Staff of General Canby, at the Army Headquarters in Santa Fe. The message read as follows:

"The Colonel will give you all the news. How is Ordnance Unit? Lt. Pike is dismissed. Stanton is captain of organization. They all go up on the lakes. I am glad to serve captain before Lt. Hanson. Fighting like the dickens yet.
In haste,
Cantain"

The captain could have been referring to the Glorieta Pass, where, apparently, the Union Army was already doing battle with the Confederates. The colonel mentioned in the message could very well be Colonel Gallegos. I am under the assumption that Lieutenant Colonel Nicodemus contacted Colonel Gallegos to "get all the news" as requested by the captain. How did the note end up in the service record of Colonel Gallegos? Probably Lieutenant Colonel Nicodemus gave the note to him for his records.

The Battle of Glorieta was fought on March 8, 1962, and the Rebels were defeated. The Apache Canyon Battle occurred on March 26, 1862, and two days later ended in a decisive victory for the Union Forces. The Texans were compelled to retreat to Santa Fe, where preparations were made for the withdrawal of their entire force from the Rio Grande Valley to Fort Bliss in Texas.

The Civil War in New Mexico was actually over in August, 1862, when the last of the Confederates were routed by the California Column. The California Column was organized by Colonel James H. Carleton. It consisted of five companies. The column had the double objective of preventing a Confederate invasion of California and helping to expel the enemy from Arizona and New Mexico.

Source: Story written by Fidel S. Gallegos. Courtesy of Stefanie Joan Gallegos.

Don Antonio Bernabe Gallegos:

Figure: Antonio Bernabe Gallegos. Courtesy of Stefanie Joann Gallegos.

Nov. 26, 1868. Bernabel Gallegos, son of Jose Guadalupe Gallegos and Josefa Gutierrez with Maria Juana Gutierrez, dau. of Juan Pablo Gutierrez and Josefa Martin from Las Colonias. Spon: Jose Miterio Rael and Antonia Aranda.

Source: Hispanic Genealogical Research Center of New Mexico Marriages, Anton Chico La Yglesia de San Jose April 1857-December 1940. P.26

Don Fidel Gallegos:

Figure: Left to Right. Top, Aunt Cleo Gallegos, Cleofitas Madrid from San Ignacio [grandma], Aunt Josefina Gallegos Ulibarri, bottom Fidel Gallegos [grandpa]. Courtesy Stefanie Joann Gallegos.

Bautize Abril 30, 1871 a Fidel Gallegos hijo lejitimo de Bernabel Gallegos y de Juana Gutierrez de Las Colonias. Padrinos: Antonio Gutierrez y Atanacia Gallegos. Source: [N.M. Baptisms Anton Chico La Yglesia de San Jose 1857-1897 p.157].

Politics:

Fidel Gallegos our Representative for the District of Guadalupe County listed #13 and address as Colonias.

Figure: Home of Fidel Gallegos. Courtesy of Stefanie Joann Gallegos.

Colonias the home of Fidel Gallegos, a farmer, a blacksmith, with humble beginnings who served in the House of Representatives after being elected Nov. 6, 1929. Fidel stood up against the New Mexico Land and Livestock Co. that saved the Anton Chico Land Grant.

The big corruption issue with T. B. Catron; N.M. 1st U.S. Senator and Santa Fe Ring caused Anton Chico Land Grant losses.

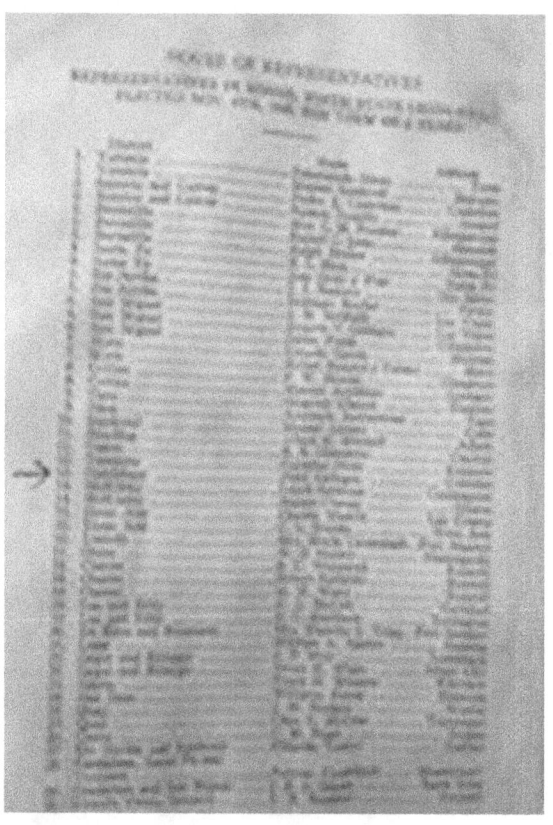

Source: Laws for the State of New Mexico, Ninth Regular Session 1929. House of Representatives in House Representatives Elected Nov. 6th, 1928, for Terms of 2 years. Courtesy Stefanie Joann Gallegos.

Figure: Left to Right. Cleo, Josephina, Portana, Adela [Max Sisneros mother], Ernestina, and Amelia. [daughters of Fidel & Cleofitas Gallegos]. Courtesy of Stefanie Joann Gallegos.

Figure: Left to right. Maximiliano Sisneros I, Francisquita Ulibarri, Isabelita, Manuel Sisneros. Courtesy Myria Trini Mandrel.

Figure: Maximiliano Sisneros II. Courtesy Myria Trini Mandrel. Figure: Adela Gallegos, Max Sisneros. Courtesy Myria Trini Mandrel.

Figure: Manuel Baca and Portana Gallegos. Courtesy Stefanie Joan Gallegos.

Figure: Left to Right. Bernabe Sisneros, Fidel S. Gallegos, Teodoro Gallegos. Courtesy of Stefanie Joann Gallegos.

Fidel S. Gallegos:

Figure: Fidel S. Gallegos at the gravesite of Colonel Jose Guadalupe Gallegos at San Jose in Colonias, N. Mex. Courtesy of Stefanie Joann Gallegos.

Fidel Silvano Gallegos was born on 5/19/1927 to 4/11/2015. His parents were Fidel Gallegos and Cleofitas Madrid Gallegos. Fidel S. served in World War II, the Korean conflict. He retired from the Naval Reserve at 60 years of age. And retired from BLM employment.

Fidel S. was a brilliant writer but most important to him was Anton Chico Land Grant and recognized all the ongoing hardships and problems which he wrote about.

Beginnings of Anton Chico Land Grant Committees:

The Rico's [rich] from the Rio Grande were grazing the Anton Chico grant and by 1869 the people met and appointed a committee to manage the affairs of the Anton Chico Land Grant. The first committee was Pascual Baca, Mariano Lucero, and Candelario Rael. Pascual Baca served as a commissioner until his death in 1899.

The second committee that followed was Bernabe Baca, Edwardo Martinez, and Jose Pablo Sandoval. This committee dealt with Henry M. Atkinson New Mexico's fraudulent Surveyor-General. Atkinson in his capacity to acquire grants common land for himself was an incorporator of four cattle companies. Atkinson used homesteads and land grants for grazing their herds.

By 1876 a new survey was ordered since the General Land Office decided that the 1860 survey was in error. Atkinson met with two committee members from Anton Chico, <u>Eduardo Martinez</u>, and <u>Jose</u> <u>Sanchez</u>. The committee requested the United States Patent of the Anton Chico Land Grant, but the committee received a letter introducing officials in the General Land Office in Washington D.C. [Michael J. Rock 1980-89].

Martinez and Sanchez were at the General Land Office on Sept. 14, 1877, representing the people of Anton Chico with a power of attorney along with their 460 signatures requesting the patent.

Again, Martinez and Sanchez renewed the application on March 10, 1879; this time 560 resident signatures appointing the two men to represent them. A final request was made by Martinez and Sanchez. On August 23, 1879, they were denied because the resurvey hadn't been approved.

In 1879 Atkinson used the technique of getting three surviving heirs which was used in Tierra Amarilla William B. Stupp began in 1879. Interest was conveyed to T.B. Catron, Judge H. Waldo, C. Gilversleeve, and L. Sulzbacher the attorney's way to gain control of Anton Chico Land Grant was manipulating and transferring eighteen deeds from three of Manuel Rivera heirs although they couldn't have acquired any interest because in 1827 none lived in the Anton Chico Land Grant.

It was determined that the grant belonged to the residents of Anton Chico and all rights should have been protected by the Treaty of Guadalupe-Hidalgo.

The resurvey was finally approved in the spring of 1882. Anton Chico Land Grant was issued its patent on March 27, 1883. By April 20th <u>Pascual Baca</u> and <u>Candelario Ulibarri another committee</u> applied with the Surveyor General Atkinson for the patent, but Atkinson told them that the patent to the Anton Chico Land Grant was his!

After twenty-two years Atkinson was no longer in the picture and now Thomas B. Catron had bought the cattle company. <u>The new committee for the Anton Chico Land Grant was now Fidel Gallegos Sr.</u> [father of Fidel S. Gallegos] <u>Florencio Garcia, Jesus Maria Rivera, David Marquez, Fernando Baca, Liberato Aragon,</u> and <u>Santiago Parras</u>. This committee sued the company to quiet the title of the grant. The attorneys for the committee were Charles A. Speiss and Stephen B. Davis Jr. nine years of court and the final decree was September 6, 1915. The customary fee to the attorneys should have been one-third but 100,000 acres were paid off to them and deeded to the U.S. Senator and speculator T.B. Catron 35,000 acres for relinquishing the cattle company claim. The residents of the Anton Chico Land Grant were declared the owners. [Michael J. Rock 1980-89].

By 1925 the residents of Anton Chico Land Grant had another loss to deal with when the Preston Beck owners filed a suit because of the overlap of Anton Chico Grant on the Preston Beck Grant. The Courts decision favored Preston Beck and the people of Anton Chico lost 120,000 acres.

Preston Beck Grant is north of the Pecos River and is about 36 miles long and 15 miles wide at its widest point. The residents of Dilia lost their right to Anton Chico Land Grant because Dilia is north of the Pecos River and in the Preston Beck Land Grant. There were six members on the Board of Trustees, but it was reduced to five to comply with the court's decision by ousting the member from Dilia. [A story of Anton the Chico Grant by Fidel S. Gallegos].

During the turmoil of the Santa Fe Ring and our 1st U. S. Senator T. B. Catron grabbing Land Grants Dilia's residents feared that the Anton Chico Land Grant would be lost. The residents in Dilia were afraid to lose their homes and farmlands and didn't wish to spend money defending Anton Chico Land Grant in the long court battle and therefore filed suit to quiet title to the portion known as Dilia, N.M. ["A Brief History of The Anton Chico Land Grant From Its Beginning Until The Present" Severiano R. Sisneros Jr.].

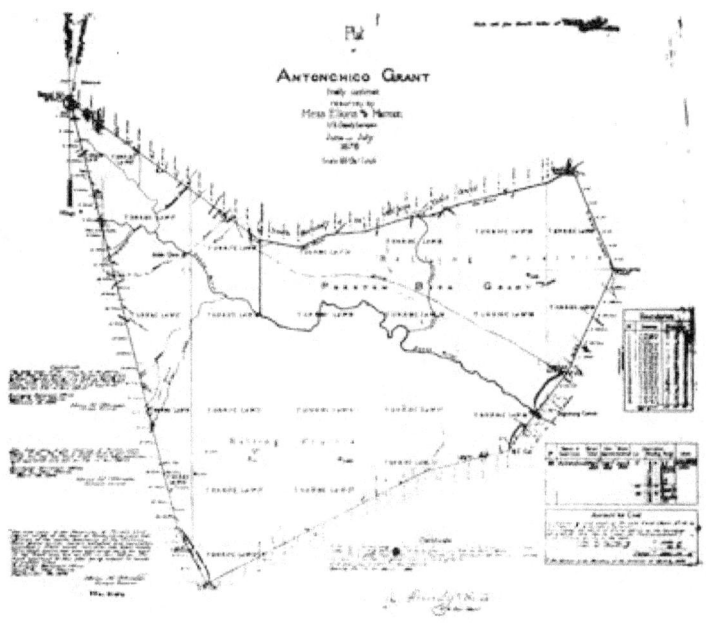

Source: Plat of Anton Chico Grant 1878, Collection of Fidel Gallegos. Courtesy of Stefanie Joan Gallegos.

Source: Writing and photo by Fidel S. Gallegos. Courtesy of Stefanie Joann Gallegos.

Figure: Cerrito in Colonias. Courtesy Stefanie Joann Gallegos.

COYOTE TRAPPING IN NEW MEXICO

By Fidel S. Gallegos

The days were getting colder. The leaves of the trees were turning yellow and were falling to the ground. The grass was turning gray, and the water on the lakes was beginning to freeze. Skunks were moving from one cornfield to another, digging their dens on the "arroyos" that led from the cornfields toward the Pecos River, as farmers were hauling their corn from the cornfields. A few 'coon tracks were seen here and there. It was the last day of November - the time I had been waiting for!

I didn't do so well trapping coyotes the previous year, but this next year I was hoping to do better. I had been reading trapping books written by professional trappers; and as I had had a little experience trapping coyotes the year before, this made me more optimistic.

I had colored my traps two weeks in advance and were now ready to be set. The lure and the bait were already in the packsack. My gloves and the trap covers were still on the clothesline airing.

I spent part of the night in front of the cheerful fireplace reading the FUR-FISH-GAME magazine. After reading for a few hours I went outside to bring more wood for the fireplace. The "mesa" where I had intended to set my traps was now illuminated by the rising moon. Coyotes had just started their yelping notes.

After eating breakfast the next morning, I saddled my horse, and was on my way. I rode up the river toward the place where I had intended to set the traps. At last we arrived at a coyote "pass". This coyote "pass" was a narrow part of the Pecos River which lay between the "mesas". The only outlet was a steep trail over the summit of one of the "mesas". It was not necessary for me to use the trail as the river was now dry, and I could go up the river as far as I wanted to go.

There are many trees growing on both sides of the river at this point which their leaves make a good trap covering. There are "mesquite" trees growing here too. We know that where there are "mesquite" trees, rats are abundant, and where there are rats there are coyotes. Many skunk tracks were seen on the sand which led from the "mesa" to the cornfields which meant that the air was going to smell differently in a few days.

Looking toward a "manzanita" tree, I saw coyote tracks which showed a good spot to set a trap. Using a dry stick I dug a hole on the ground, placed the bait inside the hole and added a few drops of lure in the back of the hole and covered the bait slightly with dirt to resemble the work of a coyote. Next, I dug a bed for the trap and the grapple, covering both trap and grapple with dry leaves.

On and on I went up the river making a "set" here and a "set" there. The sun was climbing higher and higher while the shadows of the "mesas" were disappearing.

All my "sets" were mostly "dirt hole sets". As I climbed to the other side of the river, I discovered a horse carcas near a trail. Coyote tracks were plentiful here. Again I set another trap. Finally, I came to an "arroyo" that came out from the "mesa" into the river. Coyote tracks were plentiful here which meant that coyotes were using the "arroyo" as their main trail when coming out from the "mesas" to their hunting grounds down in the valley. I set another trap on the river about twenty feet from the mouth of the "arroyo". After setting a trap here, I crossed to the other side of the river to a narrow trail that led from the canyon to the river. Here I made a trail set with my last trap. The sun was now sinking in the horizon.

2

Turning my horse toward the Spanish village, I galloped leaving my trapping ground behind. Above stretched the brilliant sky of New Mexico. It was dark when I reach the village. The new moon sheded its feable rays over the "mesas". After giving my horse his supper I went inside the house to get mine.

After eating a hearty breakfast the next morning, I was on my way to collect the crop. The first "set" held nothing; the next "set" the same. Finally, I came to the "arroyo" where my sure-fire "set" was. The first thing I saw were pieces of the trap cover scattered around. It didn't take me long to find the marks of the trap's grapple. The marks led me up the "arroyo" into a canyon. As I was climbing the "arroyo" to the other side I heard a noise. The noise was that of a chain. My heart began to beat now. Yes, at the very end of the canyon was the coyote standing with feet wide apart. It was a beauty. The 22 roared leaving only an echo on the deep canyon. The other traps held nothing.

Day in and day out I rode my trapline, sometimes finding one coyote; sometimes nothing. When the trapping season ended, I had trapped forty coyotes, four bobcats and twenty-five skunks. To me this was an excellent "catch" for it was my second year of trapping.

Word Vocabulary (Webster's International Dictionary):

Adobe - Brick made of earth or clay dried in the sun. A house built of adobe.

Arroyo - A water-carved gully or channel.

Manzanita - Western evergreen shrub.

Mesa - An isolated flat-topped natural elevation more extensive than a butte and and less extensive than a plateau.

Mesquite - A spiny deep-rooted leguminous tree or shrub.

3

Source: A 3-page writing by Fidel S. Gallegos. Courtesy Stefanie Joann Gallegos.

Figure: Left to Right. Bernabe Sisneros, Max Sisneros Sr., and Teodoro Gallegos. Courtesy of Stefanie Joann Gallego.

Don Teodoro Madrid:

Figure: Teodoro Madrid born April 1863; Emilia Sena born June 1872. Courtesy Stefanie Joan Gallegos and Myria Trini Mandrel.

Children: Benjamin born Oct. 1889, Cleofitas born Aug. 1891, Margarito born Feb. 1900. Source: 1900 Census La Pintada, Guadalupe, N.M.

Maternal grandparents of Teodoro Gallegos.

Figure: Teodoro Madrid Letter. Courtesy of Stefanie Joann Gallegos.

Figure: Teodoro Madrid Letter. Courtesy of Stefanie Joann Gallegos.

Teodoro Gallegos:

Figure: Merlinda Veronica Monreal Martinez fr. Albuq. and Teodoro Gallegos fr. Colonias [4-18-1935 to 5-11-2018]. Courtesy of Stefanie Joann Gallegos.

Figure: Teodoro Gallegos. On a bronc at las Colonias. Courtesy of Stefanie Joann Gallegos.

Rodeos:

Teodoro raised money for repairing la capilla de San Jose en Colonias with rodeos. A project that was important to him.

Figure: Teodoro Gallegos. Courtesy Stefanie Joann Gallegos

The Rocking Wildcats:

Figure: Left to Right. Robert Pohl [sax], Richard Sanchez [drums], Fidel S. Gallegos [band leader/ sax], Teodoro [Ted] Gallegos [lead vocals/ lead guitar. Fidel and Ted / brothers. Courtesy of Stefanie Joann Gallegos.

Ted's band "The Rocking Wildcats" along with Robert Pohl on sax. Robert Pohl the brother of Gloria Pohl and mother of Lorenzo Antonio and the "Sparx" all musical artists. [Stefanie Joann Gallegos, personal communication, Nov. 7, 2020].

Blas Hoehne:

Figure: Blas Hoehne World War II. Courtesy of Nancy Ann Hoehne Flores.   Figure: Nancy Hoehne, Blas Hoehne. Courtesy of Nancy Hoehne.

Blas:

During certain occasions when resolving mysteries and problems Blas would say, "O pues ay esta' la chingadera". Blas was an honest and outspoken man.

"Las diecisiete", Blas said, upon arrival at the Y intersection of I-40 and highway 84. Blas explained, "17- miles to Anton Chico and 17- miles to Santa Rosa".

Upper Antón Chico:

Conditions were set forth to the settlers of the Anton Chico Land Grant: work together on projects of common benefit, irrigation ditches, building a church, pass muster by having guns and or bow and arrows. The comanche attacks were unbearable and by 1827or 1828 Anton Chico was abandoned.

By March of 1834 fourteen men resettled Anton Chico. Including Bernardo Ulibarri and Mariano Aragón survivors from the first settlers attempt. The alcalde constitucional from San Miguel del Vado Juan Martin carried out the verbal orders. Reimposing the three conditions that were attached to the first possession. The report and Juan Martin's signature was witnessed by Manuel Rivera. Rivera did not receive any land because he didn't move back to Anton Chico after the abandonment of 1827or 1828. [Michael J. Rock 1980-89].

The Texas Expedition in 1841-42 was accompanied by George W. Kendall. Upon arrival in Upper Anton Chico their observation was the little hill overlooking the Pecos River.

The Sangre de Cristo church was used for services and the bell rang during those times, but they also rang the bell to announce a fandango [dance]. The village square was built with adobe houses and doors fronting the inner side of the plaza serving as a fort with a population of two or three hundred.

The low adobe houses with flat roofs and the two-room home which had floors of dirt and no windows but had a strong door built in the front of the inner part of the village that was built in the high table lands enclosed in the valley. Especially for protection from the cold winds and the Indians that made their attacks from time to time.

The houses had fences made of adobes and the two-room house was the house of the "First Family". The first family house had no chairs or table and neither did they have forks or knives. Juan Martin the first Alcalde was introduced by the first family to the Americans.

Men were concealed in coarse blankets which made it hard to tell whether they wore clothes underneath. The women and girls were slightly clothed, and some of the children were naked.

The men inquired about the available shops and soon were able to spend their few shillings.

Red chile ristras hung in the outer walls of the adobe houses. The Americans thought the ristras were for decoration and to their surprise the chile punished some of the Americans with swelling to the mouth and face when they chose to add the condiment to their food.

The next day a fandango was held in the evening. Shirt collars and fronts were made of stiff drawing paper. Hunting coats, leather leggings, and heavy boots were worn by some Americans. Arms were not allowed but some did carry a revolver or a bowie knife. Bad refreshments were sold for good money. The Señoritas rolled cigaritos for their partners. Singing, dancing, and laughing went on until the morning. [Stanley, F., The Anton Chico Story (New Mexico) Story: 1975].

Pascual Baca and Tomas Gallegos vs J. B. Salpointé

Filed for record on the 4th day of December A.D. 1894 and duly recorded this 5th day of December A.D. 1894

W B Iddenacy
P.C. and Ex Officio Recorder.

Sepase que yo Pascual Baca por y en consideracion de un peso traspaso y entrego a su Señoria el arsobispo J. B. Salpointé de nuebo mexico la capilla de la sangre de cristo en anton chico en el Condado de San Miguel y Territorio de nuebo Mejico para que su señoria la tenga para siempre el y succesores como propiedad legitima de la iglesia catolica apostolica Romana, dicho traspaso lo ejecuto en birtud de que soy un agraciado lejitimo en la merced de Anton Chico y en dicha merced se alla ubicado dicha capilla fundada por mis abuelos agraciados en la dicha merced y ademas en birtud de ser una comicion guardiana de dicha merced firmado junto conmigo Don Tomas Gallegos secretario de dicha comicion dicho traspaso es libre de todos en barasos y si los ubiere esta escritura la pondra en quieta y pasifica pocesion y son sus linderos de dicha capilla por el norte un arroyito que esta a tras de dicha capilla por el oriente la asequia madre por el sur beynte llardas de patio, por el poniente se estiende asta el solar del finado Pablo Martines dicho traspaso lo ejecuto y lo firmo junto con dicho secretario en presencia de un juez de pas esta dia 11 de mayo año del señor de — 1886

original   Pascual Baca (SRCS)
                Tomas Gallegos secretario
        Fernando Baca
                Juez de Pas del precincto no
3. Condado de San Miguel.

Source: Sangre de Cristo Church document, Upper Antón Chico. [Courtesy Mary Sanchez Baca].

Figure: School in Upper Anton Chico.

School:

Georgia Ackerman taught school in Upper Anton Chico around 1918. Her living quarters were at Rosario Jaramillo's house in Upper Anton Chico. Georgia rented a room from the Jaramillo family since the school was walking distance from Rosario Jaramillo's house.

Georgia had visits by James Abercrombie in Upper Town. Bringing her chocolate candies as a gift. Sharing candy with Rosario's kids. They were the lucky ones. [Bobby Jaramillo, personal communication, September 17, 2021].

Figure: Back side of School in Upper Anton Chico. Courtesy Ray Lucero.

Figure: Filimon Martinez [Graduation at Upper Anton Chico School. Courtesy Rosemary Urioste.

Filimon Martinez was born in 1916. The son of Gabriel Martinez and Dionicia Lucero Martinez.

Doña Dionicia Lucero Martinez:

Figure: Left to Right. Dionicia Lucero Martinez, Cecilia, and Dolorita. Courtesy Rosemary Urioste.

El Jardin:

Doña Dionicia maintained her garden with the essential and favorite vegetables green chile, calabacitas, and corn. Saving the seeds from the previous year and planting chile seeds in early spring to get an early start of the almasigo [early potted plants] was important. During the month of May, she put her plants in the garden plot then began the chore of watering and hoeing during the summer. Hoping that rain will come for the river flow. Arturo Lucero said, "May 13th is the last day to plant Chile."

Harvest began sometime in August. Chile was a part of everyone's meals. The first batch of green chile on the table was something to look forward to.

Then came the preserving of the harvest which meant roasting the chile over the wood stove, peeling it and hanging it out to dry. Finally putting it in a flour sack in the dispensa [storeroom] for winter meals.

The calabacitas and apples were cut into rueditas [circular slices]. Then the rueditas were laid on a screen or towel. Drying calabacitas out in the sun until they were ready to be stored in a flour sack for later winter meals.

Rosa de Castilla:

While fishing I got a swelling and rash on my skin. I went to see Dionicia for treatment thinking that perhaps I had touched poison ivy and got a rash.

Dionicia crushed yellow petals from the wild rosebush and mixed them with Vaseline. The ointment was for the swelling and the rash of poison ivy.

Ventosa's:

Dionicia got a candle and then lit it and placed it on the patient's stomach. She then put a drinking glass over the candle. Once the flame went out, she began to run the glass thoroughly over the stomach until the air suction was gone. Dionicia lit the candle again and continued the person's back following the same process with the ventosa [glass and candle treatment] used for empache, [swallowing gum, or eating uncooked cake mixes or dough] which was believed to be the intestines been stuck together. Then finally pulling the glass off from the stomach and back area creating a suction which was believed to treat the empache.

Figure: Graviel Martinez, Dionicia Lucero Martinez.

Figure: Left to right. Cecilia, Dionicia Lucero Martinez. Courtesy Rosemary Urioste.

Figure: Maria Martinez [Sister of Alvirez], Courtesy Rosemary Urioste   *Figure: Ramon Castillo. Courtesy Rosemary Urioste.*

Figure: Dionicia Lucero Martínez, Rosemary Urioste.   Figure: Left to right. Ismael, Jose Gertrudis, Macario Lucero. Courtesy Rosemary Urioste.

Figure: Left to right. Andres Lucero, Lucy Chavez, Rufina Lucero.   Figure: Left to Right. Rosemary Urioste, Gregoria Martinez.

Figure: Julia Martinez, Rosemary Urioste. Courtesy Julia Martinez.   *Figure: Left to right. Dionicia Lucero Martinez, Huberto Sisneros, Courtesy Rosemary Martinez.*

Figure: Left to right. Nerio Lucero, Cecilia Lucero, Rosa Lucero, Andy Lucero.   *Figure: Julián Ramírez [son of Julia & Leo Ramírez]*

Courtesy Rosemary Urioste.   *7/29/1983. Courtesy Julia Martínez Ramírez. Figure:*
Gregoria Martinez. Courtesy Rosemary Urioste.

Nerio:

José Sandoval a WWII veteran had his home at los ranchitos a little tiendita and his home located at what is now known as the Encarnación Sisneros place.

Manuel Morales lived across the road and was preparing to help with the pig matanza[slaughter] and was sharpening his knife.

Thirty-three year old Jose was now home doing his farm and ranch chores. He got the rifle to slaughter the pig and while turning the corner of the house his wife warned him about the 22-rifle and the dangers involved. She told him, "cuidado con el rifle" "el diablo se puede meter"! He hit the loaded rifle on the floor and it went off. The bullet hitting Mr. Sandoval in the stomach then ricocheted to his head. Mrs. Sandoval was right the fatality of her husband had just turned into her worst nightmare.

Nerio heard about the accident and ran barefoot all the way to los Ranchitos from Upper Antón Chico and arriving there before anyone else. He was a curios eleven year old boy. [Nerio Lucero, personal communication, September 8, 2019].

Manuel Morales:

Figure: Manuel Morales II. Clorinda Sandoval Morales. Courtesy Larry Morales.

Figure: Left to Right. María, Clara [cuatas] Porfilio Martínez, Florencio Martínez [hermanos]. Courtesy Rosemary Urioste.

Figure: Filimon Martinez.

Figure: Joseph Martinez Courtesy of Rosemary Urioste.

Figure: Lola Martinez. Courtesy of Rosemary Urioste.

Figure: Evelyn Martinez. Courtesy of Rosemary Urioste

Figure: Gregoria Martinez. Courtesy of Rosemary Urioste.

Figure: Left to right back. Rosemary Urioste, MaryAnn Martinez Armijo, Becky Gallegos, Patsy Martinez, Gregoria Martinez, Manuel Martinez, Julia Martinez Cuevas. Courtesy Rosemary Urioste.

Figure: Left to Right. Isabel Martinez and Benito Sisneros. Figure: Left to Right. Dolores Martinez, File Martinez, Phillip M. Gaby M., Paul M. Courtesy Rosemary Martinez.

Compact tree of Jose Nerio Lucero

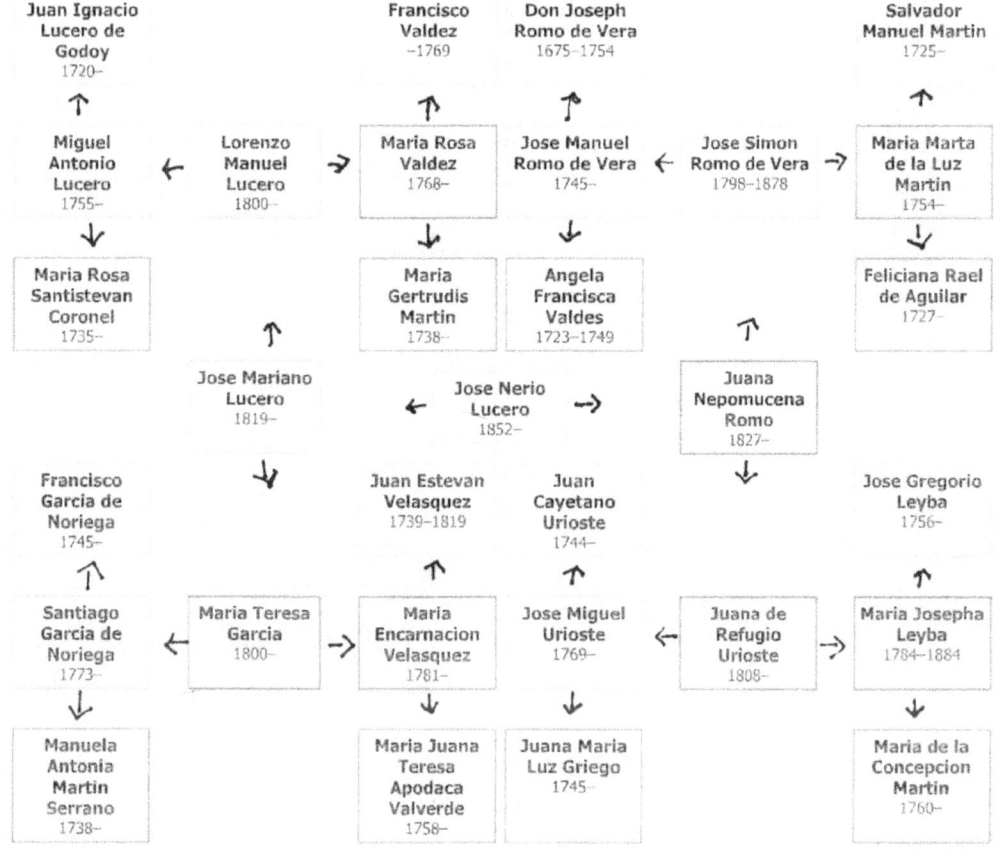

Source: HGRC Compact tree of Nerio Lucero.

Figure: Nash Sisneros, Rosemary Urioste, Huberto.   Figure: Nerio Lucero, Maxine Lucero. Courtesy Rosemary Urioste

Figure: Left to Right. Manuel Martinez, Linda, File Martinez.   Figure: Left to right. Julia Martínez, Mario.

Courtesy Rosemary Martínez.   Picture taken 7/1997. Courtesy Julia Martínez.

Figure: Jenny Lucero [daughter of Andres and Rufina].   Figure: MaryAnn, Duke Armijo. Courtesy Julia Martinez.

Figure: Left to Right. Perfilio Martinez, Native American, Maria Aragon, [twins] Clara Aragon. Courtesy Rosemary Urioste.

Figure: Alfredo Ulibarri, Tina Martínez Ulibarri.

Figure: Left to right. Joseph Ramirez [son of Julia], Tamara. Courtesy of Rosemary Urioste.

Figure: Ramon Urioste, Rosemary Urioste. Courtesy Rosemary Urioste. *Figure: Ramon Urioste. Courtesy Rosemary Urioste.*

Figure: Gregory Madero. Courtesy Rosemary Urioste. Figure: Mario Fernando Madero Maestas. Courtesy Rosemary.

Doña Lola Sisneros:

Figure: Lola Sisneros. Courtesy Rosemary Urioste. *Figure: Left to right. Nash Sisneros, Ruby Sisneros Peña, Huuberto Sisneros. Courtesy of Rosemary Urioste.*

Figure: Dilia Duran Sisneros, Fidencio Sisneros [Son of Lola Sisneros]. Figure: Left to Right. Ignacio Sisneros and a friend. Courtesy Rosemary Urioste.

Figure: Carlos Sisneros Wedding. Courtesy Rosemary Urioste.

Figure: Left to Right. Alfredo, Tina, Isabel Sisneros, and Queta Martinez Lucero. Courtesy Rosemary Urioste.

Figure: Left to Right. Ray Lopez [father of bride] Abenancio Sisneros [known as Cascarias], Ambrosia Lopez Sisneros, Mrs. Ray Lopez, Lola Sisneros [mother of groom]. Courtesy of Rose Mary Urioste.

Figure: Left to Right. Cecilio Castillo, Manuel Duran, Magdalena Sisneros, Bersabe Castillo. Courtesy Rosemary Urioste.

Figure: Left to Right. Cecilio Castillo, Bersabe Castillo, Julia Sisneros Aragon, Manuel Aragon.   Courtesy Rosemary Urioste.

Figure: Left to right Gregorita Martinez, Maria Sisneros.

Figure: Rachel Margaret, Rosemary Urioste. Alex Sisneros, Courtesy Rosemary Urioste.

Figure: Feliciano Sisneros. Courtesy Rosemary Urioste.

Figure: Mr. Mrs. Alejandro Sisneros [1/2 brother to Abenancio].

Figure: Bersa, Father Ramon Castillo, and Cecilio Castillo. Courtesy Rosemary Urioste.

Figure: Top Bersabe Castillo. Left to Right Clara Martinez, Maria Martinez, Ramon Castillo [Priest] Courtesy Rosemary Urioste.

Figure: Left to Right Manuel Martinez, Berna Jaramillo, Cecilia, Lucero, Dionicia Lucero Martinez.

St. Joseph's Catholic Church/Nuns:

Tire Trouble in The

Missions Around Anton Chico

1925-1930

With Appreciation for The

Victory Noll Sisters

Who Taught and Lived

The Gospel with The

People Of Anton Chico.

Father Charrie:

Figure: Father Charrie's fatal car accident. Courtesy Agneda Aragon Pino.

The fatal car accident that took Father Charrie's life in Springer. Miguel Ulibarri [brother of Josefina Ulibarri Aragon] accompanied Father Charrie and remained paralyzed. Beatrice Maestas Ulibarri [sister to Tomas Maestas] was also in the accident. Beatrice was born in Cuervo, N. M. on 9-16-1884 and lived to be 101 years old. The parents of Beatrice were Jesus Maria Maestas and Ascencion Maestas. Jose and Beatrice Ulibarri's children Mela Ulibarri Segura, Josefina Ulibarri Aragon, Jose A. Jr., and Domingo Ulibarri. Beatrice raised Carlos Aragon Jr.

Figure: Father German Charrie in Anton Chico around 1918-1941. Buried in front of Iglesia de San Jose.

El Cerrito de La Tierra Blanca:

El Cerrito de la tierra blanca is on the Cueva del Padre Road with very distinct white dirt and white rock. This Cerrito has a wooden Cross that father Gaete and some volunteers helped put on the top. Former renta de Nick Cordova.

Cerrito del Pedro Miguel:

This Cerrito is on Dahlia Road to the left. A wooden Cross also put at the top of the Cerrito with the help of some volunteers and Father Gaete.

Pat Garrett:

Figure: Left to right. Unidentified, Pat Garrett was born 6-5-1850 to 2-29-1908. Courtesy Agneda Aragon Pino.

Beatriz Maestas Ulibarri [Mamaita] was given Pat Garrett's picture. Beatriz is the daughter of Ascencion Lucero and Jesus Maria

Maestas. Beatriz Maestas was married to Jose Basilio Ulibarri [Agneda Aragon Pino, personal communication].

Figure: Beatriz Maestas Ulibarri [Mamaita] [born April 19, 1885] daughter of Ascencion Lucero and Jesus Maria Maestas. Courtesy Agenda Aragon Pino.

Figure: Left to Right standing. Mela Ulibarri Maestas, Manuel Segura, Bride Josefina Ulibarri Maestas Aragon, sitting Groom Carlos Jacobo Aragon. Courtesy Agneda Aragon Pino.

Figure: Left to Right. Bobby Segura [son of Cristobal], Daughter of Bobby, Beatrice Maestas Ulibarri, Mela Segura Maestas Ulibarri [dau. of Beatrice], Cristobal Segura [son of Mela], baby granddaughter of Bobby. Courtesy Agneda Aragon Pino.

Page 230. Abril 19 de 1885.
Bautize a *Beatriz Maestas*, hija legitima de Jésus Maria Maestas y de Ascencion Lucero, d Pajarito. Padrinos: Claro Maestas y Juana Lucero.

Source: New Mexico Baptisms, Anton Chico La Yglesia de San Jose, April 1857- December 1897.

Anton Chico:

Figure: River Crossing Anton Chico to Tecolotito. Courtesy Mary Sanchez Baca.

Antón Chico to Tecolotito:

This is the river crossing after 1857, and the San Jose Catholic Church was already built south of the Pecos River. The flood of 1929 had destroyed the metal truss bridge which was the crossing from Anton Chico to Tecolotito. [Reymundo Maestas, personal communication, May 27, 2007].

The trees in the picture have lots of leaves therefore it is possibly summertime. Seven wagons are crossing the Pecos River with some thirsty horses after the families leave church.

Families from Tecolotito baptized and attended to their church obligations at San Jose Catholic Church in Anton Chico.

Bridge to Anton Chico:

Note the high dirt road to the right which lead to the bridge crossing, and to the bottom of the dirt runway appears to be a straight object below the riverbank that could have been part of the bridge structure. Grandpa Manuel Lucero recalled crossing the acequia of Tecolotito and crossing the river at the Puente to Anton Chico. "The bridge that was taken by the 1929 flood" said, Reymundo Maestas.

The old dirt road remains today but has a lot of brush and growth on the roadside.

The Six Men Up Front:

There are three men on horseback and Tio Telesfor's white macho [a burro and mare cross and male offspring] is pulling the second wagon. Benito Baca [grandson of Telesfor] once said, "yo quisiera unmacho". Tio Telesfor respondio, "pues yo tenia unmacho blanco". And in front of the wagon pulled by the macho is my grandfather Juan P. Lucero on his horse the same mafrico [wild with no brand, mustang] with a wild mane and the white saddle bag. A very unattractive and notable horse that grandpa rides on many family pictures.

The horse and cowboy to the right of Juan P. Lucero is Luis Otero [brother-in-law]. The cowboy in front to the right of the wagon facing Anton Chico is Tio Telesfor. Every cowboy had his own horse.

Western Attire:

The men are all dressed up for a special occasion. These men wore their typical cowboy clothes a white shirt at times and a vest. The hat is usually another trademark for each man. Andres Lucero [El papito] wore a suit jacket most of the time and his typical hat. Papito holds the reins in the front wagon. Great grandmother Petra Chavez Lucero passed away 2-25-1929.

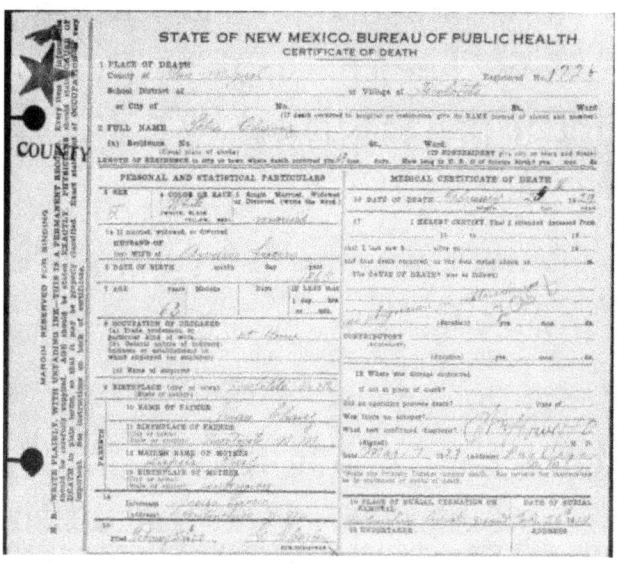

Source: State of New Mexico Certificate of Death Petra Chavez.

Baptism:

Virginia Lucero Otero is holding the baby dressed in white and wearing a bonnet. She and Papito baptized Andres Lucero 6-28-1930 his parents are Jesus Lucero and Estefana Sisneros.

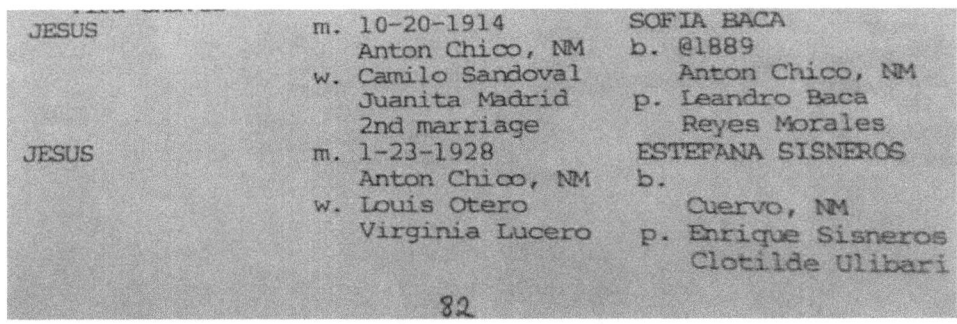

Source: San Jose Catholic Church Anton Chico, New Mexico Marriage Records.

Figure: Andres Lucero, Rosa Romero.

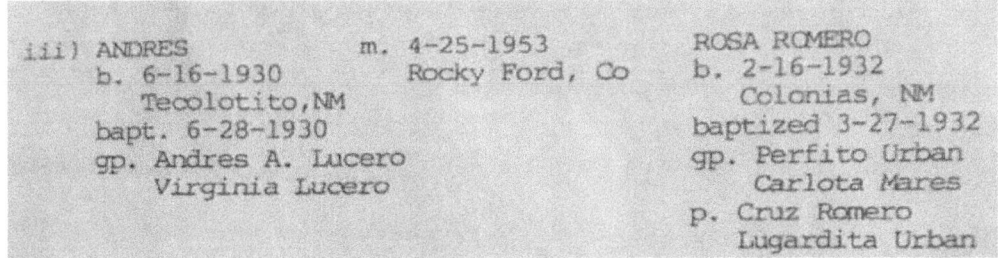

Source: San Jose Catholic Church Anton Chico, New Mexico, Marriage of Andres Lucero, and Rosa.

Two umbrellas are held by the family up front. The six Lucero men were usually together. Two other wagons with families are holding umbrellas.

Figure: Left to right on horseback. Silviano Lucero, Jesus Lucero, Luis Otero, Telesfor Lucero [on white macho], Juan P. Lucero [on mafrico]. Front Andres Lucero [Papito] children unidentified.

Figure: Tecolotito to Anton Chico River crossing. Courtesy Beverly Lucero Baca.

Grandpa Juan en su Mafrico:

Figure: Left to right. Telesfor Lucero, Juan P. Lucero [at el rancho at la Union]. Courtesy Virginia Quintana.

Grandpa Juan admired all horses which is now quite clear since in the early 1900's the horses available were the mafricos. Those horses were not very big and often had a big head. Grandpa helped with the mafricos that the family captured especially "El Alazán de Los Luceros" after all he was a good race horse. El Alazán a mafrico was small but ran some good races, because he ran very straight never losing any time.

As grandpa got older I saw him admire the horses that my father bought. The horses were now bigger with more muscle and better blood lines, versus the mafricos which grandpa had seen throughout his life.

Figure: Left to right. Unidentified horse, Juan P. Lucero Sr., El Prieto. Courtesy Juanita Everett Donelson.

My father Juan Lucero Jr. was a tracalero [a man that liked to wheel and deal] and on this one deal he bought a black horse, El Prieto. Edwardo Lucero Sr. from Anton Chico sold El Prieto to my dad. Edwardo had two horses, the second horse he sold to his brother-in-law. During the training grandpa Juan determined that El Prieto had a good running time, and my father raced El Prieto from there on.

The racetrack in Las Vegas was where Walmart now stands. On a Sunday afternoon El Prieto and other horses ran a race in Las Vegas. During the race a man got on the track that day while the horses were running, and the man was trampled.

Dad lost interest in racing El Prieto, but my grandfather, Don Juanito, loved horses and he became the owner of El Prieto. Racing El Prieto in Dilia, El Chapel, and Las Vegas.

Grandpa cared for his horses by feeding them grain and alfalfa. Exercise was a daily routine for his horses and taking them for a ride to the sand at the arroyo del Tecolote.

En El Chapel Don Juanito raced his horses con los Chapulines or raced con Don Jenaro Garza en el Chapel.

Don Jose Nestor Garcia:

Figure: Jose Nestor Garcia. Courtesy of Isabel Salas Barela and Lorraine Barela Pohl.

Figure: Left to Right. Narciso Ulibarri [Uncle Joe's bro.] Groom Abel Sena, Bride Eloisa Salas, Maid of Honor Victoria Salas Rael, [sitting] Nestor Garcia, Alejandra Lucero Garcia [Grandma Terecita's Parents]. Wedding 6/28/1948. Courtesy of Isabel Salas Barela and Lorraine Barela Pohl.

Source: El Llano, Guadalupe County 1910 U.S. Census.

Figure: Left to Right. Alejandra Garcia, Francisco Garcia [son] Jose Nestor Garcia. Courtesy of Isabel Salas Barela and Lorraine Barela Pohl.

Francisco Garcia in World War II:

Francisco Garcia was a World War II veteran born 1909-1976. Francisco was inducted to the Army March 26, 1941, in Santa Fe, N. Mex. and trained at Fort Bliss, Texas. His military occupation was with the gun coast artillery, then transported to the Philippines Campaign in Aug. 27, 1941.

Francisco was in the Japan conflict and landed in the Philippines. There he was to participate in the beginning of the fight. Francisco and another soldier opted to back off and hide instead of surrendering since the other American soldiers hadn't arrived. He and his partner did not want to be taken captive by the Japanese. The two hid until the other Americans came.

Decorations:

Francisco was decorated and was cited for the distinguished Unit that had an American Service with the Crown Star Asiatic Pacific Theatre Campaign. Francisco got the Bronze Star for the heroic meritorious deed performed in armed conflict. His departure and separation of service July 19, 1945, with a little more than four years' service and an Honorable Discharge.

Source: Ancestry Francisco Garcia, 7/18/1944 "War Records Library Museum of N.M. Historical Society of N.M."

Source: Ancestry Enlisted Record and Report of Separation Honorable Discharge.

Don Zacarias y Terecita Salas:

Figure: Left to right. Terecita Garcia Salas, Zacarias Salas. Courtesy of Isabel Salas Barela and Lorraine Barela Pohl.

Zacarias Salas was born Nov. 2, 1895, and enlisted in the U.S. Army June 5, 1917, as a Pvt., Company C, Military Unit 134 Infantry, in U.S. Army WWI. Zacarias departed on Oct. 13, 1918, from New York on the Khiva.

sourcee: Ancestry Military, Registration Card Zacarias Salas.

Returning on the U.S.S. Sibonney from Brest, France on June 27, 1919, and arriving on July 5, 1919, in New Port News, Virginia.

Source: Ancestry, The USS Siboney. Zacarias Salas transportation from France.

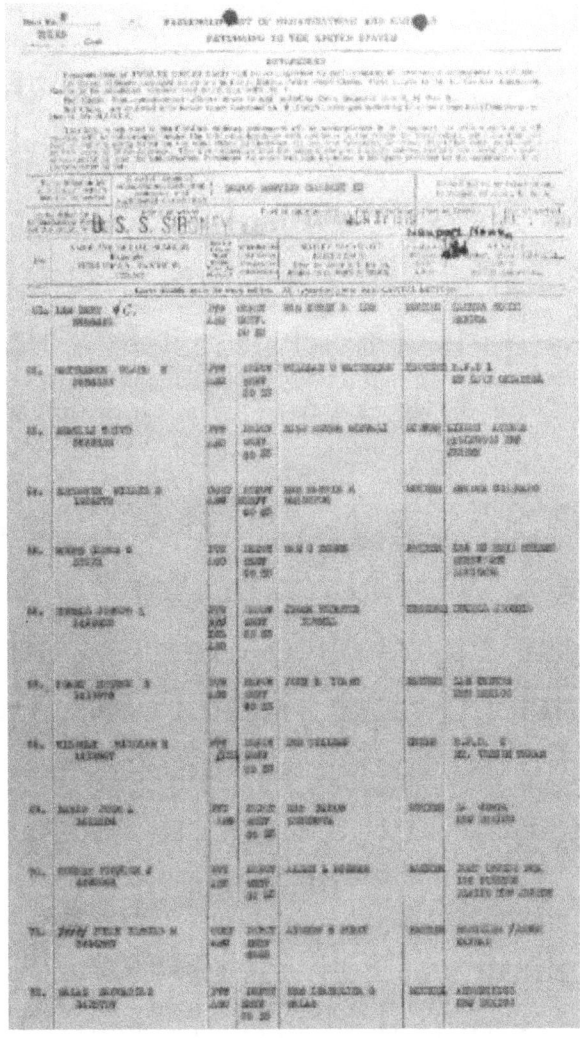

Source: Ancestry, Zacarias Salas Records of Military Records,

Community Service:

    Zacarias was active in the community even though his education was limited to grade school as was for most back in those days. Zacarias understood the people when serving as President of the Anton Chico Land Grant Board of Trustees. He knew the people well and during decision making he used logic and spoke up.

Acequias:

The acequia Madre was dug by horse and escrepa [dirt scrape and scoop]. Men with shovels and hand tools were used for manual labor as required when the land grant was to settle.

"Anton Chico has a well-established acequia system since the 1840's" as quoted by the Carlsbad Project Water Operations. [Source: Carlsbad Project Water Operations and Water Supply Conservation FEIS].

Acequia water rights were vested to the Tecolotito Community Ditch or West Ditch at Anton Chico, the lower end which is Upper Anton Chico with a priority date of 1836 to divert sufficient water of the Pecos River through the ditch and for the use in Tecolotito and Upper Anton Chico. Proper irrigation of the respective acreage of land and acreage in San Miguel and Guadalupe Counties.

The Hormigoso Community Ditch, or East Ditch at Anton Chico has vested rights of a priority date as of the year 1844. The right to divert sufficient water of the Pecos River by the means of the Hormigoso Community Ditch, or East at Anton Chico, to irrigate the acreages of land properly in Guadalupe County.

Source: Fourth Judicial District of the Territory of New Mexico, County of San Miguel. "Juan Marquez et al., vs Agapito Sandoval et al., Civil Docket 4149 p.p. 112, 126.

A dam for Dilia was built prior to the current one a few hundred yards upstream using brush and materials gathered from the surroundings. Some materials are still visible in the river.

The WPA built the Tecolotito dam and completed it 4-7- 1932.
[Reymundo Maestas, personal communication, May 27, 2007].

Zacarias was mayordomo and helped with the Acequia business also. A board was needed to manage the acequia. The very important job given to the mayordomo for the upkeep of the acequia which requires management and a lot of physical labor.

During the Spring the Tecolotito, Hormigoso, and Bado de Juan Paiz ditches stop the water flow from the Pecos River. The acequias dry out during the given time depending on the weather and snow fall. Allowing the acequias to dry out for spring cleaning. During the time of Zacarias's service in the acequia all the cleaning was done physically with men cleaning out excess dirt, and silt by shovel. Overgrown brush along the banks also had to be chopped with the ax and taken out of the ditch.

In Tecolotito and Plaza de Arriba don Vicente Jaramillo was Mayordomo for many years. His duty was to gather the acequia cleaning crew and to watch the parciantes [landowners with water rights] with reminders to shut water gates or to fine the parciante. Sometimes Vicente found a parciante watering out of turn and he simply shut the water gate.

Each landowner provided help during acequia cleaning. Frank [Cuaresma] Sisneros worked in the acequia choosing his helper Junior Tenorio. Juan asked Junior to skip school and help with the acequia cleaning. Don Vicente the mayordomo marked a vara [32 in. to 44 in.] length of the acequia per helper. Don Vicente carried the vara as he went ahead marking the designated marks and the men moved along cleaning the acequia. Most landowners paid for the helpers, but some families provided their helpers.

Source: Acequia token for days work.

Figure: Blessing by Father Charrie of Tecolotito Atarque [dam] 4-7-1932. Courtesy Ray Lucero.

Don Santos:

Zacarias's brother Santos Salas was questioned by others, "que hay Dios"? He responded, "creo que sí". Zacarias, "dice que si ay". Él le reza a ese hombre.

Then they asked, "que hay diablo"? And then he responded, "creo que sí". "Dicen que lo han visto, creo que lo han visto".

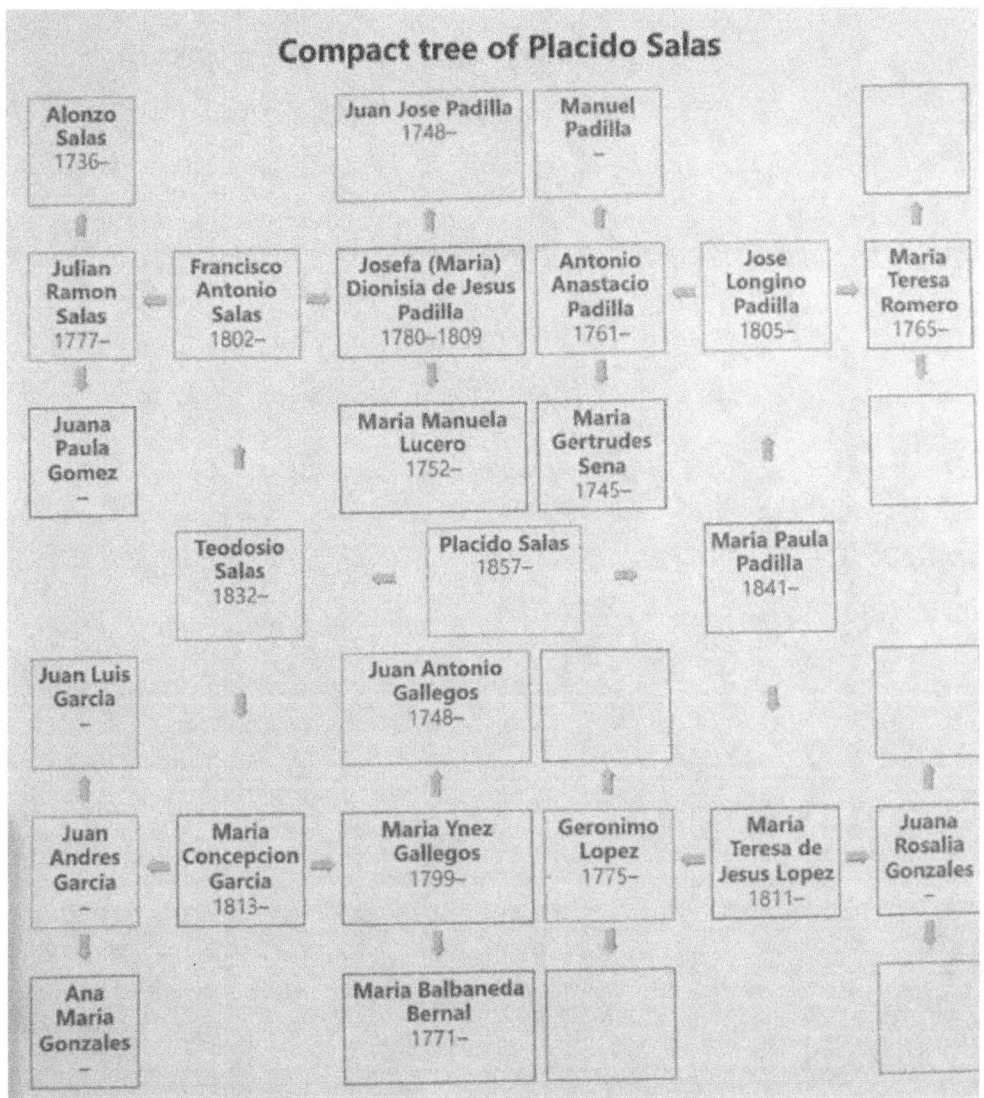

Source: *Compact tree of Placido Salas Hispanic Genealogy Center of New Mexico.*

Source: U.S. Federal Census Transcriptions. 1900, San Miguel County Territory, La Liendre and State of New Mexico.

El Fileto:

Figure: La Carcelita en El Fileto. Courtesy of Joe Romero.

Figure: La casita de Filimon Romero en Fileto. Courtesy Joe Romero.

Figure: Left to right. Andalecio Romero, unidentified. Courtesy Arturo Romero.

Hunting:

Andalecio Romero's favorite hunting grounds at Fileto along the Pecos River is about 12 miles upstream from Tecolotito.

Andalecio invited his friends and family on deer hunts. Ramon Lucero often went along as the cocinero [cook]. Prudencio Villanueva, Juan Tenorio, Junior Tenorio, Tío Jose Lucero, and my dad Juan Lucero, Perdomo Baltazar, and Jimmy Baltazar were some of the men on Andalecio's hunting party throughout the years.

The hunters all brought something to eat. Andalecio said, "Ay traigo un frasco con perrodos" [beans] Tío Jose brought a jar of rosas [popcorn] that didn't quite pop but was all eaten at camp. Potatoes and pan [bread] del campo were brought by the other hunters.

Prudencio Tambien se remangaba [rolled up his sleeves] and helped with peeling the potatoes and recalled his mother peeling potatoes and getting on his case for eating raw slices of potatoes.

The night was cold, but my dad Juan Lucero had very heavy homemade blankets. Junior was assigned to sleep with my dad. The blankets were heavy and there was no movement or complaining of the cold night.

Hunting throughout the day meant carrying a canteen of water if you chose to but not this hunting party because it was fine to drink water from the Pecos when someone got thirsty. Andalecio and Jimmy Baltazar got thirsty and drank water from the river. Upon meeting up to Perdomo he offered his son Jimmy a drink of water, but Jimmy wasn't thirsty, and he told his dad,

"Andalecio and I drank water from the river". Perdomo said, "No! Andalecio es como un animal no bebas de ay"!

Los Jaramillos:

Tiburcia Jaramillo Age 3, in the 1870, census born in 1867, grandma of Rick Romo born and lived at the Viandante. She was sister to Cesario, Bartolo 14, Eustaquia 18, Tomas 11, Pascual 9, Jose Felix 6, Monico, Juan C. 25, and Vidal 16, Jaramillo. Source: U.S. Federal Census 1870, Jorupa, San Miguel N.M. Territory.

Tiburcia married on Dec. 7, 1884, Juan de Jesus Olguin son of Juan Rosalio Olguin and Ines Gonzales's daughter of Juan Jaramillo and Juana Antonia Urioste from Viandante. Source: New Mexico Marriages Anton Chico La Yglesia de San Jose April 1857-December 1940.

By July 30, 1899, Concepcion Castillo, age 26 from Tecolotito son of N. Castillo and Maria de la Luz, born in Tecolotito married Tiburcia Jaramillo, age 23 born in Viandante. Source: New Mexico Marriages Anton Chico La Yglesia de San Jose April 1857-December 1940.

Atole:

The soldiers had a rock corral near the river crossing at the Viandante. There too was the Pony Express route which made it a busy river crossing.

Tiburcia sold atole [corn meal] to the soldiers. Into their canteens she poured a cup of atole for 3- or 5- cents.

By 1885, Pascual Jaramillo was 23, and Felix Jaramillo was 20, years old. Two of the Jaramillo brothers owned and operated a bar at the Viandante.

The description of a picture showed "two Jaramillo brothers dressed in black suits like that of Mormon attire along with black hats described" Ricky Romo.

[Ricky Romo, personal communication, June 16, 2019].

Doña Emilia Romero Baca and Doña Apoloñita Archibeque Romero were part of the busy settlement at la Cueva del Padre [Vicente Jaramillo's renta]. Ellas las dos ayudaban y cruzaban las mulas con carretas por el río. También molían harina. [Arturo Romero, personal communication, July 16, 2018].

Figure: Left to right. Anastacia Romero, Apolonia Archibeque Romero, Josefina Romero, Unidentified. Courtesy Arturo Romero.

TWELFTH CENSUS OF THE UNITED STATES.

SCHEDULE No. 1.—POPULATION.

State: New Mexico
County: San Miguel
Township or other division of county: Precinct No 39
Name of incorporated city, town, or village, within the above-named division: El Tecolotito
Supervisor's District No.: ~~110~~
Enumeration District No.: 108
Sheet No.: 5
Page: 146 A

Enumerated by me on the 14 day of June, 1900, Nestor Sena, Enumerator.

Name	Relation	Personal Description	Nativity (Person / Father / Mother)	Occupation	Education
Juan B	Son	W M June 1892 7 S	New Mexico / New Mexico / New Mexico	at school	3
David	Son	W M Apr 1894 5 S	New Mexico / New Mexico / New Mexico		
Rosa	Daughter	W F Aug 1897 2 S	New Mexico / New Mexico / New Mexico		
Fernando	Son	W M Oct 1899 7/12 S	New Mexico / New Mexico / New Mexico		
Archibeque Jose — Head	W M Feb 1844 56 M 37	New Mexico / New Mexico / New Mexico	Day Laborer 3	no no no 0 F H
Juana	Wife	W F July 1849 50 M 37 12 6	New Mexico / New Mexico / New Mexico		no no no
Brigida	Daughter	W F Jan 1882 18 S	New Mexico / New Mexico / New Mexico	at school	4 yes no no
Apolonia	Daughter	W F Apr 1884 16 S	New Mexico / New Mexico / New Mexico	at school	6 yes no no
Sotera	Daughter	W F Feb 1888 12 S	New Mexico / New Mexico / New Mexico	at school	6 yes no no
Antonia	Daughter	W F Aug 1890 9 S	New Mexico / New Mexico / New Mexico	at school	6
Eligia	Daughter	W F Mar 1894 6 S	New Mexico / New Mexico / New Mexico		0
Tresquez Bartolo — Head	W M Sept 1840 59 M 10	New Mexico / New Mexico / New Mexico	stock herder 2	yes no no 0 F H
Petra	Wife	W F May 1855 45 M 10 0 0	New Mexico / New Mexico / New Mexico		no no no
Castillo Concepcion — Head	W M May 1871 29 M 9	New Mexico / New Mexico / New Mexico	Stock herder 3	no no no 0 F H
Tiburcia	Wife	W F June 1867 32 M 9 2 2	New Mexico / New Mexico / New Mexico		no no no
Mariana	Daughter	W F Jan 1892 8 S	New Mexico / New Mexico / New Mexico		0
Reyes	Son	W M Jan 1894 6 S	New Mexico / New Mexico / New Mexico		0
Jaramillo Juan J — Head	W M June 1820 79 M 55	New Mexico / New Mexico / New Mexico		yes yes no 0 F H
Antonia	Wife	W F Aug 1827 72 M 55 17 8	New Mexico / New Mexico / New Mexico		no no no
Feliz	Son	W M Oct 1866 33 M 4	New Mexico / New Mexico / New Mexico	Stock herder 0	no no no
Monico — Head	W M May 1869 30 M 4	New Mexico / New Mexico / New Mexico	Day laborer 0	yes yes no 0 F H
Cornelia	Wife	W F Sept 1877 22 M 4 2 2	New Mexico / New Mexico / New Mexico		no no no
Miguel	Son	W M Sept 1897 2 S	New Mexico / New Mexico / New Mexico		
Sotero	Son	W M Apr 1900 2/12 S	New Mexico / New Mexico / New Mexico		
Pedro — Head	W M Oct 1874 25 M 1	New Mexico / New Mexico / New Mexico	Day laborer 0	yes yes no 0 F H
Genovieva	Wife	W F Nov 1880 19 M 1 1 1	New Mexico / New Mexico / New Mexico		yes yes no
Delfino	Son	W F Nov 1899 7/12 S	New Mexico / New Mexico / New Mexico		

Source: U.S. Census 1900 Tecolotito, N.M. San Miguel County.

Ufrendo Jaramillo:

Figure: Ufrendo Jaramillo. Courtesy Josephine Jaramillo.

Cerrito de la Mina:

 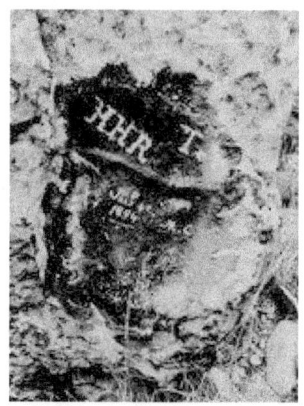

Figure: El Cerrito de la Cueva.

Source: Boulder at cave and Inscriptions 1894 M.C., HH.

This cerrito was called "Cerrito de la Cueva" or "Cerrito de la Mina" Along highway 84 past Dilia and past the Pecos River to the left and towards Colonias.

A metal track had been put in place for a little cart to roll in and out as needed to haul out dirt from the Cueva. With his burro an old man pulled the cart full of dirt as needed from the mine. He worked at the mine for a long time. The Viejo from Anton Chico mined for gold. One day he wasn't around. The Viejo's disappearance gave the people in Anton Chico the impression of a possible find during his gold digging.

Years later Arturo Lucero and Ufrendo Jaramillo were deer hunting near the Cueva and became curious about the cave. They noticed the mining equipment. The track and the carreta were still there and so that gave them an opportunity to get a ride. [Arturo Lucero, personal communication].

Figure: Left to Right. Virginio Lucero [son of Rufina & Andres L.] Ufrendo Jaramillo. Courtesy of Rosemary Urioste.

Figure: Manuel Martinez, Patsy Jaramillo Sanchez Urioste, and Patsy Jaramillo. Courtesy Rosemary Urioste.

Figure: Left to right. Emma Ortega Jaramillo, Rosemary

Figure: Left to Right. Roberto Jaramillo, Chavela Romero Jaramillo. Courtesy Rosemary Urioste.

Figure: Left to Right Manuel Martinez, Berna Jaramillo

George Jaramillo: Canción de Antón Chico

Ya salimos de Antón Chico con sus lindos materiales.

Vivan Luceros, Marquez, Carrillos y Sandovales.

Ya llegamos al Rancho Lee en los con sus hermosos jardines.

En de atacan pedos don Santiago Martinez. Dilia el Nick Hern tengo 55 años. Yo soy hombre de mis manos desde el día que yo naci. Arriba puso su nombre y abajo su apelativo. Yo soy George Jaramillo.

Source: Canción y versos compuesta por George Jaramillo. Courtesy Pacifico Romero 2/6/2019.

Don Florencio Aragon:

Figure: Left to Right. Florencio Aragon, Andrea Rael Aragon. Courtesy Agreda Aragon Pino.

Figure: Florencio Aragon and Andrea Aragon. Courtesy John Baca.

Family of Florencio Aragon and Andrellita Rael

Florencio was born about February 1835 and Andrellita was born about February 1846. They were married about 1857. Andrea Rael Aragon died September 12, 1910 in Anton Chico, NM at the age of 64 and was buried September 13, 1910. Father Gatignol.

BENIGNA A. GARCIA ARAGON
Born: March 22, 1860
Died: May 25, 1903
Residence: Anton Chico, San Miguel, NM Territory
Residence: Anton Chico, Guadalupe, NM Territory

HILARIO ARAGON
Born: January 4, 1862
Died: February 10, 1925
Residence: Anton Chico, San Miguel, NM Territory
Residence: Anton Chico, Guadalupe, NM

MARIA IRINEA ARAGON
Born: August 24, 1864
Died:
Residence: Anton Chico, San Miguel, NM Territory

ROMAN ARAGON
Born: December 20, 1868
Died: 1945
Residence: Anton Chico, San Miguel, NM Territory
Residence: Anton Chico, Guadalupe, NM

RICARDA A. GURULE
Born:
Died: September 22, 1916
Residence: Anton Chico, San Miguel, NM Territory
Residence: Anton Chico, San Miguel, NM Territory

MARGARITA A. DURAN
Born: December 1871
Died:
Residence: Anton Chico, San Miguel, NM Territory

MARIA ISABEL ARAGON
Born: May 1873
Died:
Residence: Anton Chico, San Miguel, NM Territory

MARIA ISABEL A. QUINTANA
Born: September 1875
Died:
Residence: Anton Chico, San Miguel, NM Territory

MARIA DOLORES ARAGON
Born: April 1877
Died:
Residence: Anton Chico, San Miguel, NM Territory

MARIA ARAGON
Born: February 1879
Died:
Residence: Anton Chico, San Miguel, NM Territory

Source: Family of Florencio Aragon and Andrea [Andrellita] Rael Aragon. Courtesy John Baca.

Saint Joseph's Church

Anton Chico, New Mexico

This is to Certify

That *Hilario Aragon*

Child of *Florencio Aragon*

and *Andrea Rael*

born in *Anton Chico, N.M.*

on *January 14 - 1862*

was **Baptized**

on *January 16 - 1862*

According to the Rite of the Roman Catholic Church by the Rev. *J. B. Fraget*

the Sponsors being { *Policarpio Chavez* / *Guadalupe Chavez* }

as appears from the Baptismal Register of this Church.

Page: *65*   Number: *I*

Dated *September 19 - 1972*

Rev. Aragon, Pastor

Source: Baptismal Certificate for Hilario Aragon. Courtesy Agneda Aragon Pino.

Mother side: Melquiares Sanchez and Maria Sanchez.

Father side: Hilario Aragon Jacoba Sanchez 1862-1925.

Compact tree of Florencio Aragon

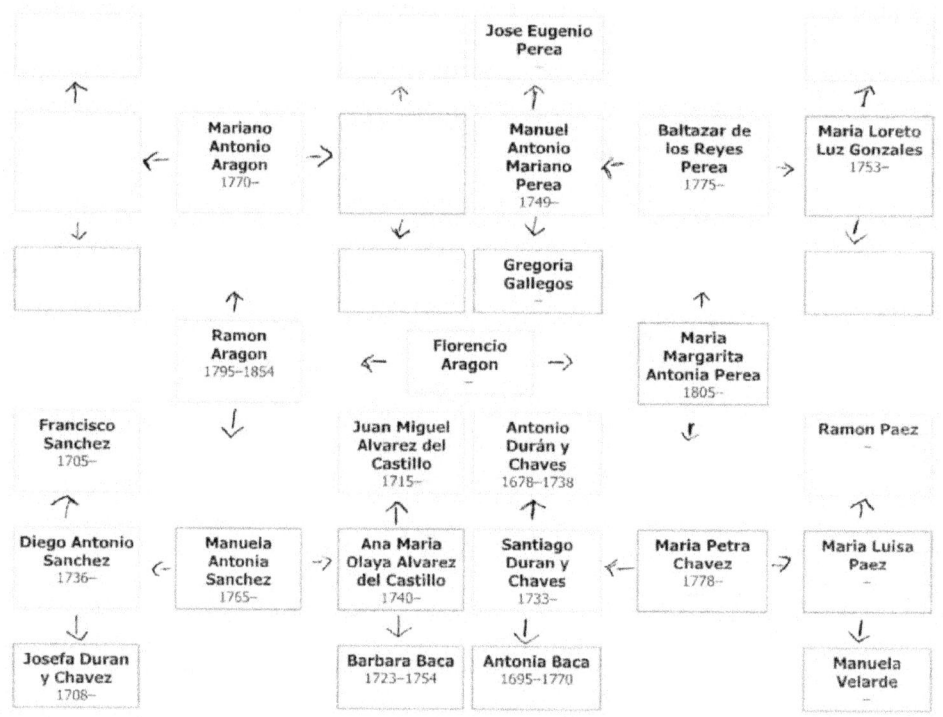

Source: Compact tree of Florencio Aragon hgrcnm.

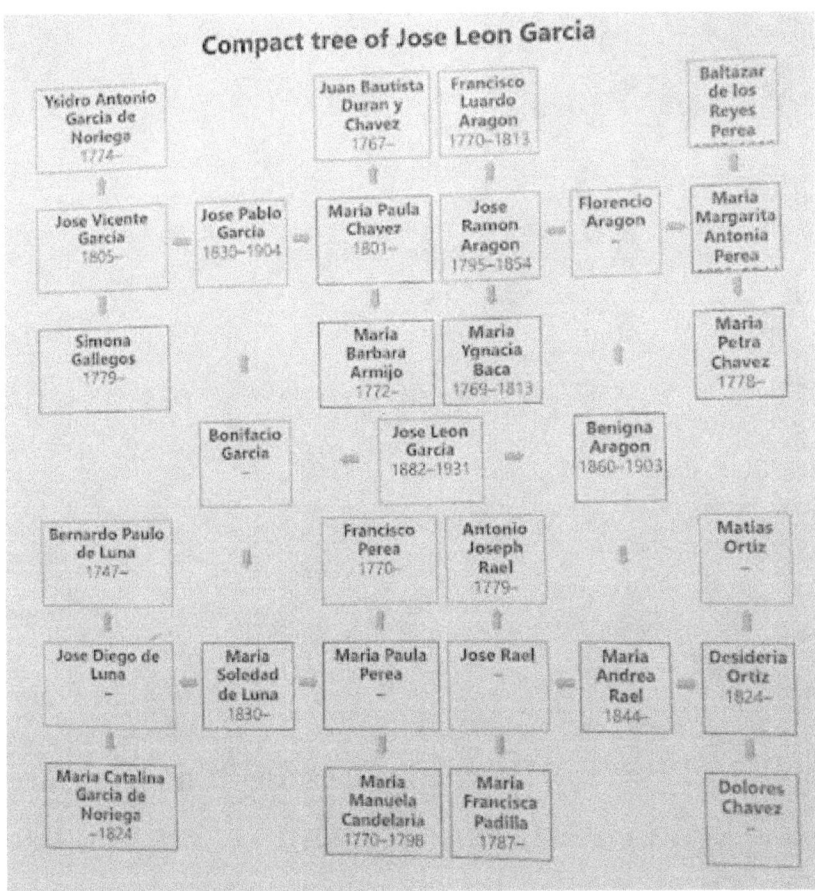

Source: Compact tree of Jose Leon Garcia hgrcnm.

Don Fernando Baca:

Figure: Left to Right standing Fernando Baca. Courtesy Mary Alice Villanueva Chavez.

Figure: Benito Baca and Bennie Baca.

Aireando el Frijol:

Arturo, Boni, and Benito Baca had been out at the Saturday night dance the weekend entertainment event. The three had been out dancing and got home at midnight ready to get some sleep.

Don Fernando was up drinking coffee waiting for the young men. The bean harvest had been completed except for cleaning out the beans. The ground surface had been swept, dampened, and the lonas [canvas] were layed out with beans which had been stepped on while the lonas were folded over the beans. The cascaras [shells] were off but now Don Fernando was waiting for aire [wind].

"Ya vino el aire ya tanto fandangeando". Tienen que airar el frijol, "dijo Don Fernando". It was windy now and late midnight but Arturo, Boni, and Benito shook the lona and the beans went up in the air and the cascaras were flying out. Shoveling the beans and shells also. The beans were finally clean. The wind blew out all the shells.

Figure: Arturo Lucero, Pedro Herrera, and Manuel Martínez. Courtesy Rosemary Urioste.

Figure: Left to Right. Unidentified, Edwardo Lucero.   Cora Lucero [dau. of Catarino Lucero]. Courtesy Rosemary Urioste.

Figure: Left to Right. Arturo Sisneros [brother to Abenancio], Vicenta Jaramillo Lucero, Ernesto Lucero. Courtesy of Rosemary Urioste.

Figure: Lorenzo Lucero. Courtesy Rosemary Urioste.   *Figure: Left to right. Unidentified Bride Rita Baca, Leroy Lucero 4/18/1960.*

Figure: Left to right. Fernando Baca, unidentified, Esteban Romero. Figure Bersabe Romero Villanueva, Chana. Courtesy Mary Alice Villanueva Chavez

Figure: Left to right. Fernando Baca. Unidentified. Courtesy Mary Alice Villanueva Chavez.

Compact tree of Atilano Baca

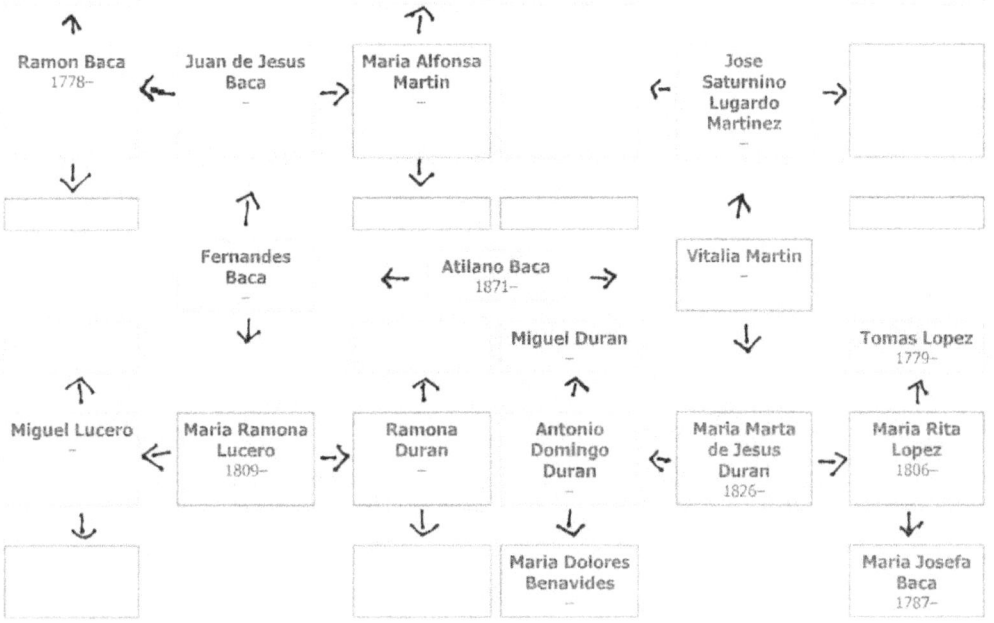

Source: *hgrcnm.org/webtrees/compact*.

Compact tree of Jose Catarino Lucero

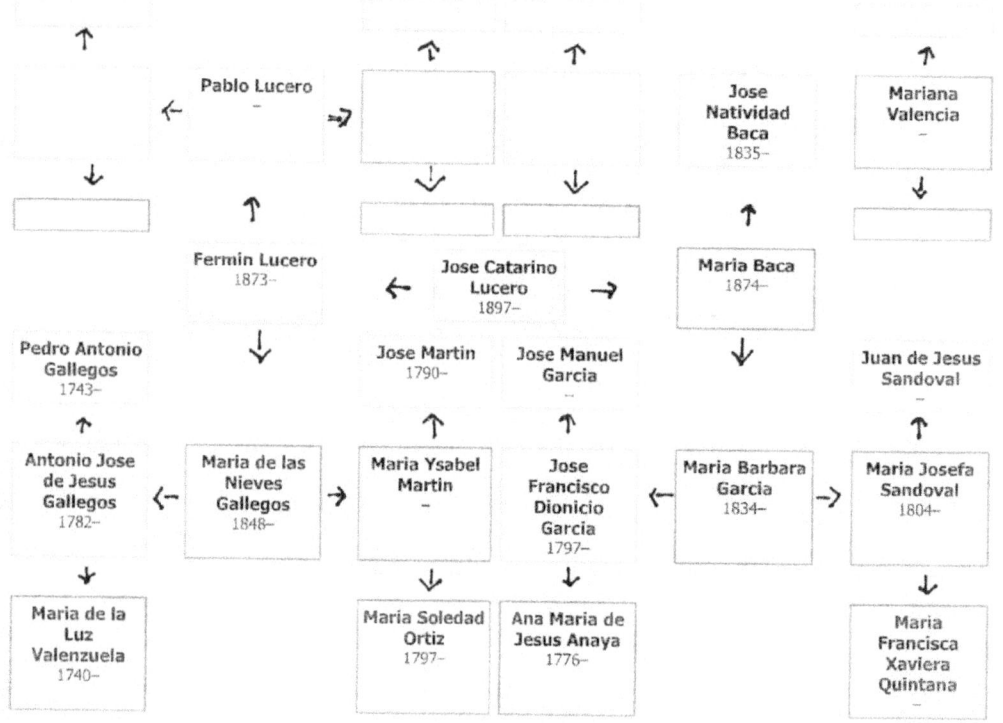

Source: hgrcnm.org/webtrees/compact.

Don Manuel Casaus:

Figure: Left to right. Sitting Uncle, , Uncle, uncle. Back standing, Great Great Grandfather Manuel Casaus, of Wilfred Bernardy, Uncle. Painting by Barbara Sandoval Bernardy. Courtesy Wilfred Bernardy.

Father – Jesus Maria Casados [born 1805]

Mother- Maria Josefa de Jesus Martin [born 1815]

son-Manuel Casaus [born 1831]

son- Jose Meliton Casaus [born 1835]

son-Teodoro Casaus [born 1837]

son-Jose Carlos Pelagio Casaus [born 1839]

Family of Manuel Casaus and Exelsa Benavides

Himself -Manuel Casaus [born 1831]

Wife- Exelsa Benavides [born 1832]

Source: hgrcnm.com

Manuel Casaus was the great great grandfather of Wilfred Bernardy. Manuel was the 1st Sheriff of Guadalupe County, serving for two terms and losing the third term election.

Teodoro Casaus lived in Dilia, N.M. at la casa grande the big house behind the capilla. Teodoro was a well to do man and funded the building of the "Sagrado Corazon" the capilla in Dilia built in 1916. The capilla was first named 'San Isidro" but Teodoro wanted to name the capilla "El Sagrado Corazon".

Teodoro was buried inside the "Sagrado Corazon" capilla in Dilia. [Wilfred Bernardy, personal communication, Nov. 14, 2022].

Papá Luis Valverde:

Figure: Left to Right. Top on truck unidentified, Papa Luis Valverde [Carmen's great grandpa] standing, Tia Adela Valverde Facio Uncle Emory, Emerenciano Campos [Carmen's Uncle], bottom row boy unidentified, blonde child probably Uncle Luis Campos [murdered in Italy after war], girl unidentified. Courtesy Carmen Campos Trujillo.

A pickup built by the family in Puerto De Luna.

Figure: Crescencia Lucero Valverde. Great Grandma of Carmen Campos Trujillo. Courtesy Carmen Campos Trujillo.

Doña Tules:

Gertrudis Barcelo is known by different nicknames. La Tules is quite fitting since it is said that she had curves. The "La" means the only one. In a disrespectful way.

La Tules was born in 1800 in Sonora, Mexico to Juan Ignacio Barcelo and Maria Dolores Herrero. The Barcelo's are traced to Gibraltar. They packed two carts pulled by mules and made the long trip to their new home in Valencia, N.M.

Tules as a young teenager made her way to Taos and then to Santa Fe. She was a beautiful red head, and she noticed some jealousy towards her amongst the Señoras.

Tules was a poor girl and she discovered that putting on make-up and combing the hair of those Señoras would be her way to make money. She earned a living by making the Señoras in high positions pretty. Tules collected her makeup materials out in the pastures. Everything Tules harvested was natural wildflowers, weeds, and any available natural materials were then made and used into her makeup collection. Napoleon Campos said, "Mamá Tules" when conversing with Carmen. [Carmen Trujillo, personal communication, March 8, 2019].

Tules may have been familiar with the "tuna blood" since the cochineal beetle that is harvested from the pear-shaped yucca has been used since the time of the Aztecs. The cochineal beetle [insect] is inside the small white fuzz. When you tear the fuzz, a tiny insect is inside and is what makes natural carmine red or crimson dye when the tiny insect is smashed.

Cochineal is used in lipsticks and dye yarn or food. The dye is a natural red which has been found to be best and not toxic or carcinogenic.

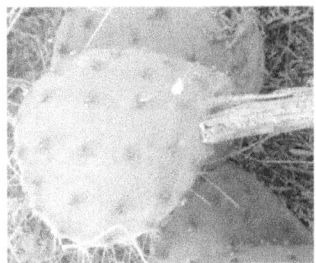

Figure: Pear-shaped yucca/ white splat is the fuzz were cochineal feeds on yucca. Courtesy Leroy Chris Tenorio.

By 1823 Tules married Manuel Antonio Sisneros although as a Latin American Spanish woman she kept her maiden name, property, legal rights, wages, and sexual urges.

By 1825 Tules lost two infant sons but with the desire to be a mother remained. She adopted Refugio in 1826 and by 15 years of age Refugio married a Mexican trader.

Tules the Madam became one of the best and a wealthy monte card dealer. A game she grew up with as a little girl began her 20-year career in 1826. Tules made money as a monte dealer and owned a brothel within two blocks at the Santa Fe Plaza that housed her ladies.

The mining camp in the Ortiz Mountains 26 miles from Santa Fe was another of her enterprising projects that found gold and mules to be profitable. Caravans of mules hauling 22 wagons of gold worth $180,000.00 enroute to Missouri. Packing of gold was done using raw buffalo and beef hides. The risk of Indian attacks remained.

James M. Giddings began his dealings with Tules and the Santa Fe trail and travels to Missouri in caravans of gold. James Giddings later married Petra Gutierres the other adopted daughter of Tules. These caravans were on the Santa Fe trail at least twice a year.

Tules was the mistress of Governor Armijo. After all she had friends with status, intellect, and power such as August de Marle the alcalde.

The residence of Doña Tules was at the intersection of Burro Alley, and Grant Avenue. The property was a nine-room home and its placita or a small square along with porches in the center belonging to Gertrudis. This established a form of security since there were no banks or police during those days and Tules and her compadres handled gold dust and coins.

At the lower Palace Avenue at Calle de la Muralla was part of the Barrio Torreon and became a part of the gambling and prostitution location. Trappers, traders, and freighters gambled and visited saloons. American officers and the poorly equipped soldiers spent or bet their money and uniform buttons too. Their stinky socks caused Tules some business.

The Lieutenant now needed a $1,000.00 loan for food and clothes for his men. Tules now had her own bank. All this made it possible to loan the Federal Government her own money.

The Notorious gambler had a Last Will and Testament by 1850 although it became legal five days before her death Jan. 12, 1852. The Will included all her property and personal belongings including a chalice and petaca [travel chest]. Many items were stolen seven months later.

Tules also planned her funeral anticipating salvation by having her mass and burial inside the church along with the first archbishop and the later archbishop celebrating her mass. An elaborate costume along with the velorio [wake] and flickering candles and alabados. Chile the main dish served and therefore the wake was called el chilito. The greater number of pasos [steps] displayed vanity instead of religious significance. Father Lujan was there to make the burial entry. No other funeral had been so extravagant except that of Archbishop Lamy. [Mary J. Straw Cook. Doña Tules. The University of New Mexico Press, 2007. P.81]

FIGURE 20. Petra Giddings Riddle (b. 1894) and Judge Santiago E. Campos (1926-2001), 1985. Granddaughter and great-grandson of James M. Giddings. Author's collection.

Source: Petra Giddings Riddle [b. 1894], Judge Santiago Campos [1926-2001, 1985. Granddaughter and great-grandson of James Giddings. Mary J. Straw Cook. Doña Tules. The University of New Mexico Press, 2007.

Petra Giddings Riddle recalled two names of men receiving passports in Santa Fe on Nov.12,1831. #72 Washington (Knox) AND #74 Washington (Jarrot-Jarret) to Chihuahua and Sonora. This was a search for the father of Rallitos although 1831 precedes the birth of Rallitos by six years. Another possibility is Washington Gerrard, a descendant of Governor Gerrard of Kentucky. Only DNA might solve the mystery.

Don Napoleon Campos:

Figure: Left to right Napoleon Campos, Luisa Valverde Campos, Carmen Campos Trujillo, Joe Trujillo. [Paternal grandparents of Carmen Trujillo]. Courtesy of Carmen Campos Trujillo.

Figure: Puerto de Luna Post Office. Courtesy Carmen Campos Trujillo.

An Arranged Marriage:

Napoleon would soon be married to 15-year-old Luisa Valverde. Luisa was a promised bride to Napoleon in an arranged marriage. Luisa didn't know Napoleon yet.

Luisa was the postmistress at Puerto de Luna. Someone at the post-office noticed Napoleon passing by and blurted out, "ay va Napoleon"! Luisa ran to the window to check out Napoleon.
[Carmen Campos Trujillo, personal communication, June 17, 2020].

Pelagio Campos:

Figure: Pelagio Campos. Courtesy Carmen Campos Trujillo.

The military excursión took Pelagio into castles made of gold.
[Carmen Campos Trujillo, personal communication, June 17, 2020].

Source: Ancestry Military Search, Pelagio Campos.

Figure: Square Deal early 1950's 201 4th street phone 3962. Courtesy of El Leon 1957.

Figure: Trinnie Campos, Pelagio [Coco] Campos. Courtesy of Carmen Campos Trujillo.

Joe Trujillo:

Figure: Sergeant Joe Trujillo, 82nd Airborne Fort Bragg, North Carolina. Courtesy carmen Campos Trujillo.

Figure: Sun n Sand Restaurant.

James Madison Gidding:

Carmen Campos Trujillo's great-great-great grandfather James Madison Giddings came from Ireland.

A cavalry man that started "Gidding's Fort". James Madison was responsible for the fort in Guadalupe County.

The fort was right along the Pecos River that originated at Agua Negra but expanded.

Uncle Orlando taught Carmen to sing "When Irish Eyes Are Smiling" and telling her about James Madison Giddings. [Carmen Campos Trujillo, personal communication, March 17, 2020].

Wilfred and Robert Hern:

Figure: Left to Right. Wilfred Hern and Robert James Hern [pic taken Oct. 1958]. Boy scouts and Nick Hern's 1957 Ford.

Figure: Left to Right. Unidentified, Wilfred Hern, Robert James Hern. Vietnam 1969. Courtesy of Robert James Hern.

Robert had served his tour in Vietnam but chose to stay and hangout with his brother Wilfred in Vietnam.

[Robert James Hern, personal communication, 2019].

Figure: Left to right. Suchiva Thim Hern, Robert James Hern. DMZ at North and South Korea. Courtesy Robert James Hern.

Don Amadeo Tenorio Sr.:

Figure: Amadeo A. Tenorio County Commissioner Guadalupe County. Courtesy Tomasito Maestas.

Figure: Casa-corral de Amadeo Tenorio. Figure: Inside casita.

The casa-corral [home and corral built jointly] was built by Amadeo at El Tomas Duran or also known as El Polinario. Inside the casita is a fireplace built into the wall. Another attached room was built to the west. The foundation is all that remains of the room. The casita is built of rock and the pitched roof was later put to preserve the casita.

Source: U.S. Federal Census. Transcriptions. 1880, Santa Fe County Territory, Galisteo and State of New Mexico.

Figure: Left to right. Mary Romo Marquez, Julia Nelson Tenorio [1st female Superintendent in Guadalupe County], Cordy Perea Sandoval [girl on desk], Lucianita Tenorio. Courtesy Mary Sanchez Baca.

Household Members: Catarino Tenorio 48 yrs. Birth abt. 1871 Head, Lucianita Tenorio 39 yrs. Wife, Nabor Tenorio 21 yrs. Son, Gonzalo Tenorio 15 yrs. Son, Lucianita Tenorio 13 yrs. Daughter, Margarita Tenorio 12 yrs. Daughter, Amadeo Tenorio 10 yrs. Son, Dorotea Tenorio 9 yrs. Daughter, Hilaria Tenorio 3 yrs. Daughter, Jenaro Tenorio 6 yrs. Son, Apolonia Tenorio 2 yrs. Daughter, Dorotea Lucero 80 yrs. Mother. *Source: 1920 U.S Federal Census Dilia, N M.*

Household Members	Age	Relationship
Manuel Tenorio	29	Self (Head) Single
Catarino Tenorio	**9**	**Son**
Roman Tenorio	4	Son

Source: Home Galisteo, Santa Fe, New Mexico, USA. 1880 U.S. Federal Census. Ancestry.

Don Ruperto y Rosita Sandoval en Dilia:

Figure: Ruperto and Rosita Sandoval home. Courtesy Virginia Sandoval Templeton.

Figure: The Store and back part was home of Virginia Sandoval Templeton. Courtesy Virginia Sandoval Templeton.

Figure: Polly Ortiz Lucero. Courtesy Virginia Sandoval Templeton.

Polly Ortiz Lucero is 16 years old and raised by Mother Rosita Alarid. Polly is waiting for the high school bus to Santa Rosa standing in front of the Amadeo Tenorio Bar in Dilia.

Figure: Polly Ortiz Lucero and Alexis Lucero wedding at the Velasquez dance hall in Dilia. Courtesy of Virginia Sandoval Templeton.

Figure: Left to Right. Virginia Sandoval Templeton, Rosita Sandoval [Dilia, N.M.]. Courtesy Virginia Sandoval Templeton.

Virginia:

> Virginia lived in Dilia and attended the school by the Morada. Her daily walk was from the Mercantile to the little school.
>
> The school had hard wood floor. The playground had a merry- go-round and swings. During recess Virginia sat on a swing but wasn't holding on tight enough and someone gave her a push. And Virginia fell off the swing and broke her arm. Amadeo Tenorio took Virginia to the hospital in Las Vegas since vehicles or transportation were difficult to find. Virginia was told that Amadeo paid the hospital bill.
>
> By the time that Virginia was 11 the parents that she knew passed away 2 days apart. Now Virginia had to leave for Denver. That was a very difficult thing for a little girl. Her friend Amadeo Tenorio and Clara Tenorio hugged Virginia and cried. [Virginia Sandoval Templeton, personal communication, December 4, 2021].

Figure: Virginia Sandoval Templeton. Courtesy Virginia Sandoval Templeton.

Figure: Julia Sandoval, Virginia Sandoval Templeton [baby]. Courtesy Virginia Sandoval Templeton.

Figure: Left to Right. Polly Ortiz Lucero, Uncle Adelino Alarid, Father Juan Sandoval, brother John Sandoval. Courtesy Virginia Sandoval Templeton.

Ricardo Alarid:

Figure: Ricardo Alarid. Courtesy Virginia Sandoval Templeton.

Can't really say it any better than my aunt:

"The last bronc has been ridden, the last calf roped, and the final roundup has come. Our "Cowboy", our beloved Grampa Ricardo has left to meet his Savior on the day of October 23, 2019."

At the ripe old age of 98 my beautiful, badass of a gramps finally traded his spurs for wings. He and his 102-year-old brother were the oldest living members of the original "Cowboys' Reunion" and had just been given the honor of Grand Marshall in their Centennial Cowboys' Reunion Parade a few years back. Here's a bit about him from an article that came out before the parade:

"Alarid will lead the Parade through the streets of Las Vegas along with a host of dignitaries made up of past-Reunion participants and officials.

"Don Ricardo Alarid is the stuff of cowboy legends," said Ron Querry, who is spearheading the centennial celebration.

Born into a family of working vaqueros in 1920 in a small village near Delia, Alarid left school after the second grade to work on the family farm. At age 16 he left home and hitched a ride to Las Vegas to find work as a cowboy.

Best known for his horse-breaking abilities, Don Ricardo remembers breaking as many as 50 horses a month for a monthly wage of $15," Querry added. "And he vividly recalls riding saddle broncs in the 1943 Cowboys' Reunion Rodeo."

I love you Grampa. See you on the other side.

Source: Ricardo Alarid. Courtesy Virginia Sandoval Templeton.

Figure: Ricardo Alarid. Courtesy Virginia Sandoval Templeton.

Miguel Gomez:

Figure: Left to Right. Miguel Gomez, Rita Ortiz Gómez [wedding], Courtesy Altagracia Tenorio Urioste.

Household Members (Name)	Age	Relationship
Jose Lucio Gomez	30	Head
Agustina Gomez	28	Wife
Andrellita Gomez	**10**	**Daughter**
Leonor Gomez	5	Daughter
Adela Gomez	4	Daughter
Jose Gomez	1	Son

Home in 1920: La Liendre, San Miguel, N.M.

Household Members (Name)	Age	Relationship
Jose Lucio Gomez	44	Head
Agustina Gomez	40	Wife

Household Members (Name)	Age	Relationship
Leonor Gomez	15	Daughter
Adela Gomez	13	Daughter
Jose Gomez	11	Son
Serafina Gomez	9	Daughter
Florinda Gomez	6	Daughter
Miguel A Gomez	**2**	**Son**

Home in 1930: La Liendre, San Miguel, N.M.

Source: Ancestry U.S. Census 1920, 1930.

Duran and Salas:

Figure: Duran's Mercantile. Courtesy Ray Lucero.

Figure: Anton Chico token. Courtesy Lee Aragon.   Figure: Anton Chico token. Courtesy of Lee Aragon.

This token was good for exchange at the store owned by Duran and Salas. The goods were for the value of ¼ days' work.

A Juan Duran and Placida operated a general merchandise store in la Cuesta in 1900 and by 1910 Census indicate they are residents of Anton Chico.

Doña Martha Baca [wife of Moises Baca]:

Figure: Left to Right. Top Martha Baca [wife of Moises Baca], Abelina Baca Esquibel [wife of Abel Esquibel], Ruperto Baca, Maria Baca [grandma of Marcos and Pacomio Ortega family], Unidentified, Ambrosita Baca [grandma of Nila Padilla Velasquez]. Courtesy of Jose Maestas.

This photo was taken at the prison while Moises Baca was serving time in prison. The unidentified girl was a standby child of a prison employee. [Jose Maestas, personal communication, July 23, 2020].

Esequiel C De Baca:

"Corrido de Esequiel C De Baca", Primer teniente Gobernador y segundo Gobernador de Nuevo Méjico. Compuesto por Abelino Urioste:

```
es el primer mexicano
criado de nuestra
Nacion Elegido y
postulado para ese Gobierno
=1=
Don Esequiel C D Baca Tomo
un destino de onor por
mattaria del del Pueblo que
Elito en la Conbencion
=2=
Democratas Vitorinos
Como Ber la Lus del dia
Su Gobenador Ganaron
Con Grande Severania
=3=
Don Esequiel C De Baca
hombre de Muncha Energia
pero dios de Termino
que pasara a Mejor Vida
=4=
```

Los Angeles California
Besita tal poseta los
medicos no pudieron
des tutuller Su Salu

=5=

Al Santario Curió
llamado de San Vicente
don Esequiel C D Baca Lia
Tormenta la Asidente

=6=

Sues posa Estova a
Su Lado y la Osabispo
en union Don Esequiel C D Baca
a Todos dando atencion

=7=

La Tarde del Mismo
dia Bien de la Capital
don Esequiel C D Baca
alli un Tren Especial

=8=

para Lugar de Las Vegas
onde lo Bon asperar
Sus Hermanos y parente
y la Rial Comunidal

=9=

Bibal Esposa y Hijos
Son dies para Limentar
Sienten a Su pobre padre
Quien les dió Susartulal

=10=

a la Casa de don Manuel
Jue onde el Sellos
Le conbenía por derecho
por Ser Hermano Mallor

=11=

Mas de 5 Mil persona
Siallavan en la ocación
asiten al Funeral
de Nuestro Governador

=12=

Munchas ofrendas
de Flores y Sieron a Su
onor aponer en el Sepulco
de Nuestro Governador

=13=

por Cuarenta y dos días
Que Nuestro Governador
pero ni Culpen a Nadien
Culpen a Nuestro Criador

=14=

Figure: Canción "Esequiel C de Baca" compuesto por Abelino Urioste. Courtesy Altagracia Tenorio Urioste.

"Corrido de Indita de Mike Archuleta". Compuesto por Abelino Urioste:

Indita de Mike Archuleta

1
A Dios le pido licencia
sentido y ligera
memoria para componer
esta Indita con paciencia
y con memoria.

2
Al joven Mike
Archuleta que este
gosando en la gloria
que los angeles del
cielo, le esten cantando
victoria.

3
Año de mil nuevecientos
67 me entiendo, murió
Miguel Archuleta
el veinticinco de
Septiembre.

4
peliando, por su govierno
una bala lo agarró
una bala rut[?]
su cuerpo lo atraveso
y en el lugar onde estava
allí su cuerpo quedó.

5
quedó solito en el llano
sin sentido y sin su
lus, ni quien le de un
baso de agua ni le
gritara Jesus.

6
Estavamos descuidados
cuando llego el telefon
de que Miguel era muerto
se nos partió el corazon
porque todos lo queríamos
porque era muy obediente
era hombre de buenas
partes y de buena educación.

7
fue distinguido su nombre en el colegio onde estaba ~~Hamold~~ H. L. un edificio nombraba

8
El dia que salio Miguel a todos nos dijo adios iva contento y alegre segun a mi parecer no sabia el probecito, que de alla no iva a volver.

9
Adios todas mis parientes y todos en general quien lo huviera sabido que mi sino iva llegar para aber echo un dino desta vida temporal.

10
quien avia de pensar Ya dios lo determino que muriera en tierra agena y en tierra agena murio.
El hombre sabe onde nace pero donde muere no.

11
Adios hermanito geo. Adios mi Elena queri- los voy a dejar solito porque ya estoy de partida.

12
no tenia padre ni madre
Miguel era guerfanito
Solo para su consuelo
tenia cuatro hermanitos
y hora por su mala suerte
lla los va adejar solitos

13
Adios mi tio Lorenzo que
me sirbio como padre
echeme la bendicion en el
nombre a mi madre
para que me alcanse el
perdon en la distra de Dios
padre

14
Dios me dio cinco sentidos
y tres potencias en la alma
ara componer ésta indita c

con pasencia y toda calma
al finado Mike Archuleta
que tenia muncha fama

15
la muerte a ninguno perdona
ni en la noche ni en el dia
lo mismo al rico y al pobre
cuando se le llega el dia

16
El que conpuso esta Indita
no es mas de un particular
si en algo me é equibocado
me deven de dispensar

17
mi nonbre se los diré pos
no acermé muy grandote
para que les quede recuerdo
de Andres Abelino Urioste

Source: Corrido "Indita de Mike Archuleta" by Andres Abelino Urioste. Courtesy Altagracia Tenorio Urioste.

Indita de Mike Archuleta:

(1)

A Dios le pido licencia sentido y buena memoria para componer

esta Indita Con pacencia y memoria

(2)

Al joven Mike Archuleta que este gosando en la gloria que los angeles del Cielo, le esten cantando Victoria

(3)

Año de mil noveciento 67 que entiendo murio Miguel Archuleta el veinte cinco de Septiembre

(4)

Peliandopor su govierno una bala lo agarro una bala lo viio su cuerpo lo atraveso y en el lugar donde estaba alla su cuerpo quedo

(5)

Que solito en el llano sin sentido y sin su luz, ni quien le de un vaso de agua ni le gritara Jesus

(6)

Estabanos descuidados cuando llego el telefonaso, de que Miguel era muerto. Se nos partio el corazon por que todos lo queriamos por que era muy obediente era hombre de buenos portes.

(7)

Fue destinguido su nombre en el colegio donde estaba en el Highlands un edificio nombrado

(8)

El dia que salio Miguel a todos nos dijo Adios iba content y alegre segun a mi parece no sabia el pobrecito, que de alla no iba volver

(9)

Adios todos mis parientes y todos en general quien tal hubiera sabido, que mi sino iba llegar para haber hecho un vecino de esta vida temporanea.

(10)

Quien habia de pensar ya Dios lo determine que muriera en tierra ajena y tierra ajena murio. El hombre sabe donde nace pero en donde muere no.

(11)

Adios hermanito George, Adios mi Glena querida los voy a dejar solitos por que yo estoy de partida.

(12)

No tenia padre ni madre Miguel era huerfanito solo para su Consuelo tenia cuatro hermanitas y hora por su mala suerte ya las va dejar solitas.

(13)

Adios mi tio Lorenzo que me sirbio como padre. Hecheme la bendicion en el nombre a mi madre por que me alcanse el perdon en la diestra de Dios padre.

(14)

Dios me diio cinco sentidos y tres potencias la alma para componer Indita con pasencia y todo calma alfinadoMike Archuleta que tenia mucha fama

(15)

La Muerte a ninguno perdona ni en la noche ni en el dia lo mismo al rico y al pobre cuando se llega el dia.

(16)

El que conpuso esta Indita no es mas de unparticular si en algo me equibocado me deben de dispensar

(17)

Mi nombre se los dire por no hacer me muy grandote para que les quede recuerdo de Andres Abelino Urioste.

Recipes:

Empanada meat filling

½ lb. boiling meat, beef, pork or tongue
1 cup raisins
c cup apple sauce
¾ cup sugar
½ cup dark syrup or light molasses
½ teaspoon cloves or less
1 " cinamon
1 " salt
½ cups piñon or walnuts
1 cup sherry wine

Empanada Dough

1 teaspoon dry yeast
2 cups luke warm water
¼ cup fat
1½ cups flour
1 teaspoon salt
1 tablespoon sugar

Roaster spice cake

2 cups sugar
3 cups boiling water
1 cup shorting
2 cups raison — 1 cup nuts
2 tsp. cinoamon
½ tsp. allspice
½ tsp. cloves
1 quart flour
1 rounded tsp. backing soda

Put sugar, shorting, raison and spices in boiling water and cook at rolling boil for 10 minutes. cool mixture thoroughly, add flour and soda and mix thoroughly. Bake at 325° for 1 hour. Remove cake pan from oven and cool thoroughly. Do not remove lid from cake while baking or cooling.

Source: Recipe by Evangelista Córdova Urioste. Courtesy Altagracia Tenorio Urioste.

Polvillo:

1qt. Boiling water.

¼ c. cold water

8 tbsp. toasted wheat flour.

Dissolve flour in cold water add slowly to boiling water & cook for about 10 min.

Sugar or piloncillo to sweeten

Source: Recipe by Evangelista Córdova Urioste. Courtesy Altagracia Tenorio Urioste.

Don Rafael Lucero:

Figure: Left to Right. Rafael Lucero born 10/24/1861 to 08/13/1942, Amada Alarcon born 09/13/1864 to 02/19/1949, baby Sisto Castillo Jr. Courtesy of Yolanda Martinez Aguilar.

    Papá Lucero light skin with green/grey eyes. Rafael was known as a notorious lawman. Mamá Amada was tall, thin, and dark skin.

Jose Rumaldo Lucero + Maria Lucia Gonzales

6 children

Juan de Dios Lucero
Birth: about 1842 24 16
Death:

Dorotea Lucero
Death:

Pedro Selestino Lucero
Birth: May 28, 1854 36 28 — Puertecito, San Miguel, New Mexico Territory, USA
Death:

Jesus Maria Lucero
Birth: June 5, 1856 38 30 — Anton Chico, Guadalupe, New Mexico, USA
Death:

Rafael Lucero
Birth: October 22, 1861 43 36 — Los Valles de San Isidro, New Mexico
Death:

Maria Luz Lucero
Birth: before October 19, 1845 27 20
Death:

Parents

Jose Rumaldo Lucero
Birth: about 1818 23 18
Death:

Maria Lucia Gonzales
Birth: before June 22, 1825 40 — San Miguel, New Mexico, Mexico
Death:

Grandparents

Gregorio Lucero
Birth: about 1795 39 22
Death:

Clara Ascension Garcia
Birth: about 1800 26 19
Death:

Andres Gonzales
Birth: about 1785 27 36
Death:

Josefa Esquibel
Death:

Family group information

Diligencias Matrimoniales
January 5, 1838
San Miguel del Bado, New Mexico, Mexico

Source: New Mexico Roots, Ltd.: A Demographic perspective from genealogical, historical, and geographical data found in the Diligencias Matrimoniales or Pre-Nuptial Investigations (1678-1869) - Chavez

Citation details: Volume VI, Page 995
Text:
1838, Jan. 5 (no. 14) San Miguel del Vado - JOSE ROMUALDO LUCERO (20), son of Gregorio Lucero and Clara Asencion Garcia, and MARIA LUISA GONZALES (12), d. of Andres Gonzales and Maria Josefa Esquibel. - Witnesses: Nicolas Casados (22), Miguel Toribio Archuleta (32), Jose Apodaca (55), all married.

January 17, 1838 **Husband:** 20 **Wife:** 12
San Miguel del Bado, New Mexico, Mexico

Source: San Miguel - Marriages - San Miguel de Vado - 12 Nov 1829-10 Nov 1878 - NMGS

Citation details: Page 17, 7th entry
Text:
17 Jan 1838 - Jose Romualdo LUZERO, single, s/ Gregorio LUZERO & Clara Asencion GARCIA, m. Mª Luisa GONZALEZ, single, d/ Andres GONZALEZ & Mª Josefa ESQUIBEL, all of this jurisd[icti]on. Test: Mig[ue]l URIOSTE & Mig[ue]l BLEA & many others.

Source: AASF, Film #39, Frame 680, 2nd entry

1841
San Miguel del Bado, New Mexico, Mexico

Source: 1790, 1793, 1803, 1823, 1829, 1841 New Mexico Censuses - Christmas, Tafoya, Olguin
Text:
Rumaldo, soldier with wife Luisa and son Jesus Maria.

1860
Los Luceros, San Miguel, New Mexico Territory, USA

Source: 1860 US census - New Mexico

https://www.hgrc-nm.org/webtrees/family.php?famid=F36547&ged=Great New Mexico Pedigree Database

Source: HGRC Jose Rumaldo Lucero + Maria Lucia Gonzales.

Record Transcription:
Us Census 1920

Household Members

First name(s)	Last name	Relationship	Marital status	Gender	Age	Birth year	Birth place
Rafael G	Lucus	Self	Married	Male	57	1863	New Mexico
Amada A	Lucus	Wife	Married	Female	55	1865	New Mexico
Florentina	Lucus	Daughter	Single	Female	27	1893	New Mexico
Jose F	Mora	Grandson	Single	Male	14	1906	New Mexico
Amada	Mora	Granddaughter	Single	Female	13	1907	New Mexico
Maximiliano	**Mora**	**Grandchild**	**Single**	**Male**	**12**	**1908**	**New Mexico**
Mercedes	Lucus	Daughter	Single	Female	8	1912	New Mexico
Clofes	Rael	Grandchild	Single	Male	3	1917	New Mexico

Maximiliano Mora's Census Details

First name(s)	Maximiliano
Last name	Mora
Relationship	Grandchild
Marital status	Single
Gender	Male
Age	12
Birth year	1908
Birth place	New Mexico
Ethnicity	American
Race	White
Can write	Yes
Can read	Yes
Father's first name(s)	-
Father's last name	-
Father's birth place	-
Mother's first name(s)	-
Mother's last name	-
Mother's birth place	-
City/township	-
County	San Miguel
State	New Mexico
Record set	Us Census 1920
Category	Census, Land & Substitutes
Subcategory	Census
Collections from	Americas, United States

Index (c) IRI. Used by permission of FamilySearch Intl

URL of this page: https://www.findmypast.com/transcript?id=USC%2F1920%2F004966457%2F00246%2F036

Source: Find my past transcript U.S. Census 1920.

Source: Marriage Certificate. Courtesy Frank Armijo.

Figure: Mary Mercedes Armijo born 1912. Courtesy Yolanda Aguilar.

Figure: Left to right. Vicente Armijo, Orlando Armijo, Ricardo (Dickie) Armijo. Courtesy Yolanda Aguilar.

Figure: Yolanda Aguilar as teenager holding her nephew. Courtesy Yolanda Aguilar. Figure: Yolanda Aguilar about 30 yrs. old. Courtesy: Yolanda Aguilar.

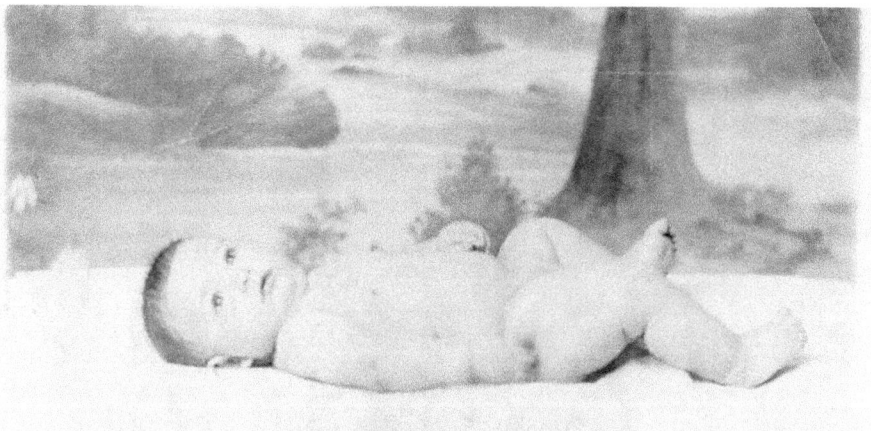

Figure: Manuel Lucero @ six months. Courtesy Manuel and Eileen Tenorio.

Figure: Left to right. Manuel Lucero, Boni Lucero. Courtesy Altagracia Tenorio Urioste.

Figure: Left to Right. Grandma Eulalia Leyba Lucero, Uncle Cresencio Lucero, Salvador Lucero, Bonifacio Lucero, Grandpa Manuel Lucero, Uncle Ben, Tia Lala Lucero Baca, and Altagracia Tenorio Urioste [1951-1952]. Courtesy Altagracia Tenorio Urioste.

Figure: Left to right. Georgia Lucero, Louisa Lucero Tenorio, front Junior, Manuel. Courtesy Altagracia Tenorio Urioste.

Doña Eulalia Leyba Lucero:

Figure: Cathedral of St. Francis, Santa Fe, N. M. Courtesy Paula Ortiz Downing.

Figure: Left to right. Altagracia Tenorio Urioste, Felipe Tenorio. Back Eulalia Leyba Lucero [Jun. 1957].

Figure: San Jose Capilla en La Cienega.

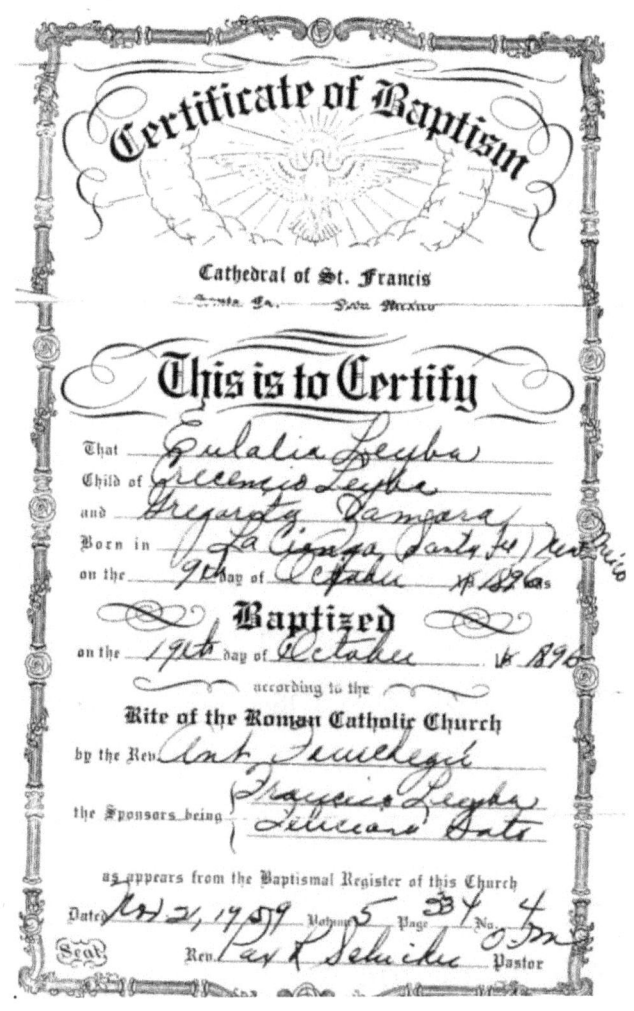

Source: Eulalia Leyba/ Baptismal. Courtesy Altagracia Tenorio Urioste.

1860 U.S. Census indicate Susano Leyba Born 1833 lived in Santa Fe [Agua Fria] with wife Juliana, and son Cresencio.

1880 U.S. Census indicate Cresencio Leyba Born 1866 age 14 lived in Los Cerrillos, Santa Fe.

1900 U.S. Census indicate Eulalia Leyba Born 1896 age 4 lived in Cienega, Santa Fe, N.M.

1910 U.S. Census indicate Eulalia Leyba age 14 lived in Las Vegas, N.M. with Uncle Petronilo Armijo and Rosario L. Armijo.

Recipe of Orejones:

Orejones [apple slices] were dried apple slices. Grandma Eulalia gathered apples in the fall. And preserved the apples by making orejones. First, she washed and peeled. The next step was to slice and then lay the slices on screens to dry. It took about three days for the apples to dry. Once they dried then it was time to put all the orejones in a cloth flour sack to allow air to continue circulating. Finally, the orejones would be stored in the dispensa [a cool room used for storage]. The apples could later be eaten throughout the winter and used for baking pies.

El Hueso Guisandero:

El hueso [a bone] that was shared within the village. It was important because times were extremely hard, and any kind of bone would give flavor to the pot of beans. Meat was a rare commodity. The bone had meat when the first family cooked their pot of beans with the bone. But in those days, it was customary to hand down the bone to another neighbor. El hueso made its rounds throughout the village.

Grandma Eulalia talked about the "hueso guisandero" She heard her elders talk about the "hueso".

Figure: Manuel Lucero. Courtesy Juan Jr Tenorio

El Viejo Mendigo:

El Viejo went around the village and was always looking for a free meal or a coffee. During the summer the common drink was cuajada [the liquid that drains from the making of cheese from fresh milk]. This was a common refreshment. The liquid could either be drank with sugar or without sugar. When the Viejo mendigo arrived at the neighbor's house they asked como la quiere usted"? "Con azúcar o sin azúcar," which was traditional when offering the drink. His response was, "una con azúcar y otra sin azúcar". [Manuel Lucero, personal communication, 1969].

Coffee Grounds:

Grandpa Manuel Lucero spoke about reusing coffee grounds since coffee was not always available when it ran out. Most families put the used coffee grounds out to dry. First, they got cardboard and then the used coffee was spread out on the cardboard. After it dried up the grounds were then put into a jar for later use during the days that there was no coffee. [Manuel Lucero, personal communication, 1969].

Butter:

Grandpa Manuel liked butter, but it required a lot of shaking movements for thickening into butter or churning. Often riding his horse and during the cool weather he tied up a jar with cream and secured it with the tientos de la silla [saddle leather ties]. The horse movements or gallops created the shaking movement needed. Upon his return home the jar of milk had become butter. [Manuel Lucero, personal communication, 1969].

Planting at El Pino:

Planting Beans, corn, watermelons, melons, and squash in dry pasture was done on the Old Nina Davis Ranch but still belonged to Manuel Lucero. After Highway 84 was built the west side was now separated from the Apache Mesa to the east.

The highway created some good water runoff to the west pasture. Grandpa Manuel decided to plant and use the water from the highway. Manuel prepared the soil and planted it then he set up a watering method to rotate the watering. During the first rain he set up for the first section of his garden to get water and then he removed the tapanco [raised platform of dirt] setting it to water the next part of his garden during the next rainfall. Everything got watered just fine. Manuel was very content with the harvest. [Manuel Lucero, personal communication, 1969].

El Pino School House:

Figure: El Pino School across from Apache Mesa on highway 84.

Louisa Lucero Tenorio attended school at El Pino as a little girl. The floors are wood in some rooms and a mud floor in the other room. The ceilings are viga and one-inch lumber. The school has had additions added.

The Lucero children also attended school at Los Montoya's and were bussed into the consolidated schools.

During a school program at Los Montoya's Cleofas C de Baca Urioste [Opa] went along to help with getting the children ready for the event. Fidel Urioste, Uralia Urioste Louisa Lucero Tenorio and Georgia Lucero attended school at Los Montoya's.
[Altagracia Tenorio Urioste, personal communication, September 24, 2019].

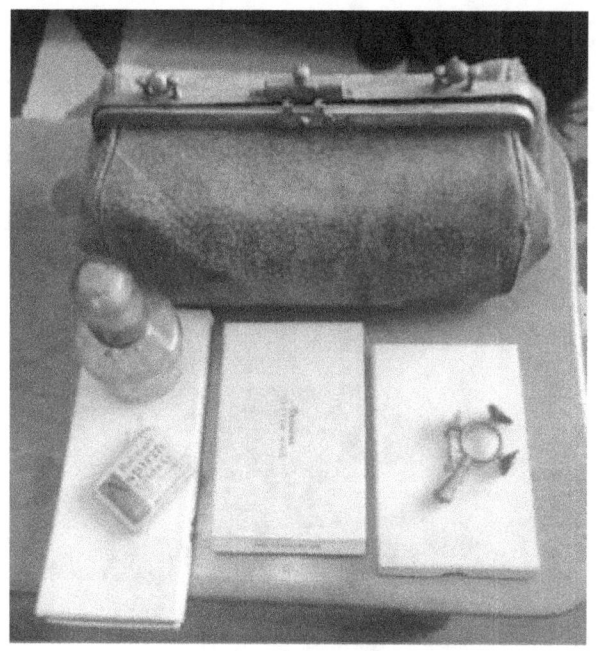

Figure: Bag and three-sided wax stamp [may have been used in the El Pino School]. Courtesy Cathy Varela.

Figure: Ben Lucero. Courtesy Altagracia Tenorio Urioste.

Figure: Left to right. Flavio Ortiz, Victoria Lucero Ortiz.

Figure: Left to right. Victoria Lucero Ortiz, Angel Ortiz.

Figure: Left to right. Antonio Ortiz, Flavio Ortiz. Courtesy Paula Ortiz Downing.

Cañon Blanco:

Flavio Ortiz lived at the casita with his parents Benjamin Ortiz and Teresita Duran Ortiz at Cañon Blanco. During the summer the boys had to build a dam with rama [branches from juniper trees] for the water to remain for the corn, calabacitas, beans, and for the plant needs. The job became tedious and hard because everytime it rained the flood washed out the handmade dam therefore giving Flavio a desire for something else. Benjamin told Flavio that the only thing he could do was to go work at the borrega [sheepherder] and that's what he did that summer. Flavio and his friend Reymundo Maestas both got jobs as sheepherders with Bond Wist in Cuervo, N. M.

Figure: Gilbert Ortiz. Courtesy Hilaria Ortiz.

Eulalia Lucero Baca

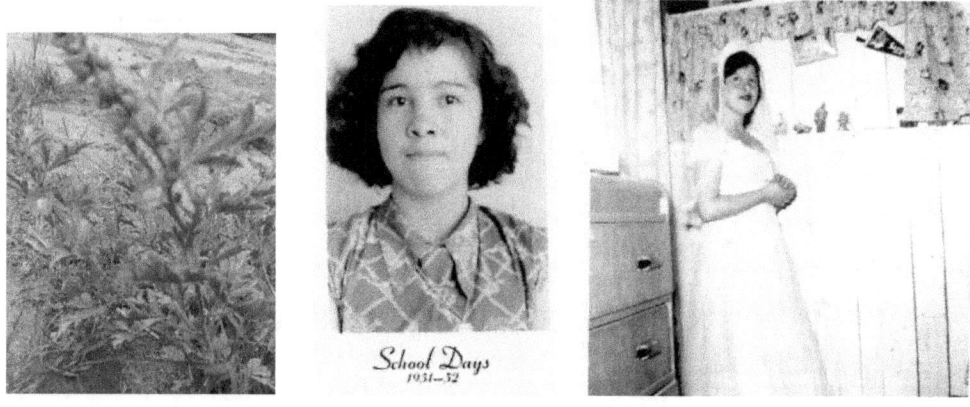

Source: yerbita de la negrita   Figure: Eulalia Lucero Baca. Courtesy Altagracia Tenorio Urioste.

Yerbita de la negrita:

These weeds blooms orange throughout June and summer. Tea can be made and used for washing hair for the prevention of hair loss or growth. [Eulalia Lucero Baca, personal communication].

Georgia's Bar "Luigi's":

Figure: Left to right. Unidentified, Georgia Lucero, unidentified.

Georgia Lucero and her friend owned "Luigi's" a bar in Pueblo, Colorado. Georgia ran the bar and later retired from the business.

Figure: Left to right. Salvador Lucero, Vitalia Sisneros Lucero. *Figure: Salvador Lucero, Georgia Lucero, unidentified. Courtesy Altagracia Tenorio Urioste.*

Snake bite:

Salvador lived in Tucumcari and worked on a farm. While working in a field cutting hay, he had the usual jam. The hay mower got jammed and wouldn't move forward without forcing the machine, so he stopped the tractor.

Un vodoque [a bunch] of alfalfa was causing a jam and Salvador stuck his hand to clear it. Pulling out as much hay as he could. He felt a prick something like a sticker, but it felt like it was more than a sticker. Salvador continued to cut hay, but his finger began to swell. Salvador told the boss about the swelling. His boss asked where he had the incident and told him at the mower jam. They checked the pile of hay and part of the snake was found. They rushed to the hospital, and he got treated for a snake bite!
[Manuel Lucero, personal communication, 1970].

Sister Betty Mora:

Figure: Sister Betty Mora. Courtesy Altagracia Tenorio Urioste.   *Figure: Sister Betty Mora. Courtesy of Altagracia Tenorio Urioste*

Sister Betty:

Uncle Joe Mora was a military man and his only child Betty spent some of her life in Vaughn with her uncle Cisto Castillo. There she graduated from high school and then went into the convent. She became an administrator and an advisor for young girls in New York and Philadelphia.

Teresa and Jose Lucero:

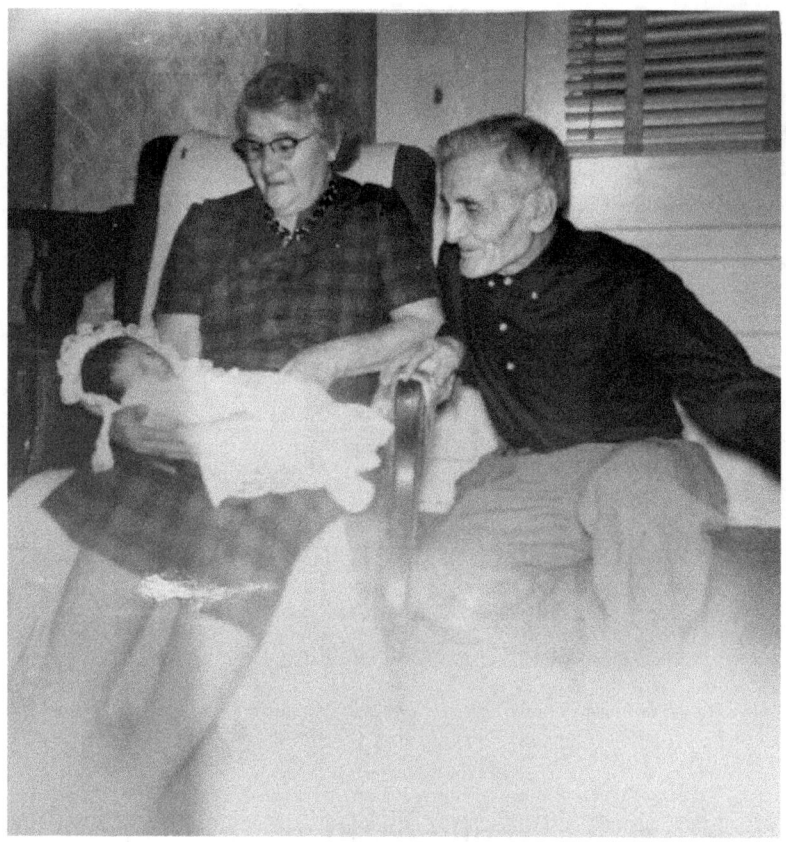

Figure: Left to right. Teresa Lucero Lucero and Joe Lucero. Courtesy Josie Ramos.

Teresa Lucero was born 1890-Sept. 9, 1985, daughter of Rafael Lucero and Amada Alarcon Lucero. Jose Lucero was born Nov. 21, 1888, to April 23, 1973, the son of Manuel de Los Reyes Lucero and Maria de Los Reyes Sandoval.

Don Andrés Lucero, "El Papito" y Abuela Petrita:

Figure: Andres Lucero "Papito" [Born 11-6-1861 to 5-22-1946] Married 9-5-1882. Petra Chavez Lucero [born 1872 to 2-25-1929]. Courtesy Leroy Duran.

Fido:

Papito had a sheep dog named Fido. [Rita Lucero Hinostrosa, personal communication, Feb. 6, 2019].

Sheep dogs were immediately brought to get milk from the goats in the corral as soon as they were born. Papito milked and poured the milk for the puppy to drink from a bowl until it was able to eat. The puppy, goats, and sheep became a family with a deep bond for one another. That's the smell that Fido recognized once he opened his eyes, and the attachment was all about goats, sheep, and Fido. Protection for the sheep was very important for

Papito's sheep when out in the pastures. Fido was now ready to chase coyotes or bobcats and protect his herd from all predators.

Figure: Andres Lucero [Papito]. Courtesy Mike Valdez.

The parents of Jose Antonio Lucero de Godoy II were Juan Lucero and Antonia Varela. Source: Origins of New Mexico Families, A Genealogy of Spanish Colonial Period. Fray Angelico Chavez Revised Edition.

Martin Lucero de Godoy
1729–1785
4th great-grandfather

LifeStory Facts Gallery Hints

When Martin Lucero de Godoy was born on February 5, 1729, in Albuquerque, New Mexico, his father, Jose, was 42 and his mother, Maria, was 36. He had one son with Maria Antonia Rosa Lujan in 1779. He died on August 5, 1785, in Cochiti, New Mexico, at the age of 56.

You • • • Ysidoro de Jesus Lucero de Godoy — **Martin Lucero de Godoy** — Jose Antonio Lucero de Godoy II / Maria Antonia Rosa Lujan — Maria Francisca Valera Jaramillo

5 FEB 1729 — Birth
Martin Lucero de Godoy was born on February 5, 1729, in Albuquerque, New Mexico, to Maria Francisca Valera Jaramillo, age 36, and Jose Antonio Lucero de Godoy, age 42.

02/05/1729 • Albuquerque, Bernalillo, New Mexico

5 FEB 1729 — Family of Lucero de Godoi-Early Records pg. 20 Martin Lucero

Record of baptism and marriage

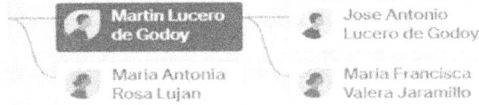

Known Issue of Antonio Lucero⁴ and Francisca Jaramillo:

A. Martin Lucero de Godoi⁵ Bp. 5 Feb. 1729 San Felipe de Neri
   Padrinos: Antonio Gonzales y Maria Lopez
   Married: Antonia Rosa Luhan (see index)

05 Feb 1729

22 APR 1752 AGE 23 — Death of father
His father Jose Antonio passed away on April 22, 1752, in Albuquerque, New Mexico, at the age of 65.

Jose Antonio Lucero de Godoy II
1687–1752

22 Apr 1752 • Albuquerque, Bernalillo, New Mexico, United States

1755 AGE 26 — Death of mother
His mother Maria Francisca passed away in 1755 in Santa Cruz, New Mexico, at the age of 63.

Maria Francisca Valera Jaramillo
1692–1755

1755 • Santa Cruz de la Canada, Rio Arriba, Nuevo México

20 NOV 1779 AGE 50 — Birth of son
His son Ysidoro de Jesus was born on November 20, 1779, in Cochiti, New Mexico.

Ysidoro de Jesus Lucero de Godoy
1779–

20 Nov 1779 • Cochiti Pueblo, Provincia de Nuevo México, Reino de Nueva España

Death — Edit

Martin Lucero de Godoy died on August 5, 1785, in Cochiti, New Mexico, when he was 56 years old.

5 Aug 1785 • Cochiti Pueblo, New Mexico

Source: Andres Lucero, Family Tree, Ancestry.

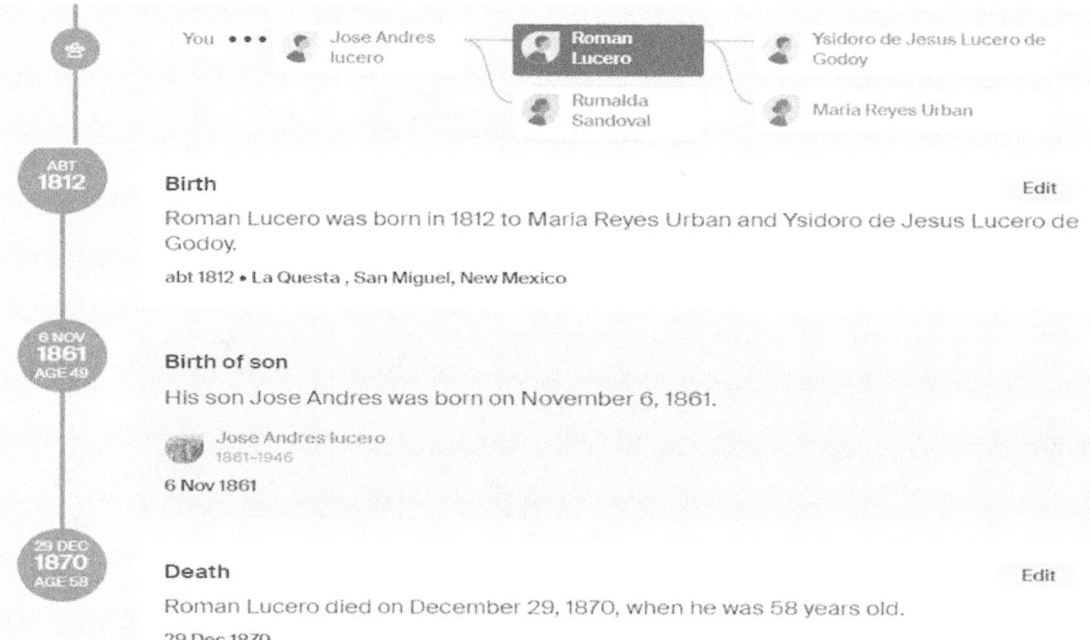

Birth — Edit

Roman Lucero was born in 1812 to Maria Reyes Urban and Ysidoro de Jesus Lucero de Godoy.

abt 1812 • La Questa, San Miguel, New Mexico

Birth of son

His son Jose Andres was born on November 6, 1861.

Jose Andres lucero
1861–1946

6 Nov 1861

Death — Edit

Roman Lucero died on December 29, 1870, when he was 58 years old.

29 Dec 1870

Source: Andres Lucero, Family Tree, Ancestry.

```
Known Issue of Antonio Lucero⁴ and Francisca Jaramillo:

A. Martin Lucero de Godoi⁵  Bp. 5 Feb. 1729 San Felipe de Neri
                            Padrinos: Antonio Gonzales y Maria Lopez
                            Married: Antonia Rosa Luhan(see index  )
```

Source: Andres Lucero, Family Tree, Ancestry.

Figure: San Felipe de Nerie en Albuquerque, N. M.

Figure: Left to right. Benigno Lucero, Andres Lucero [brothers]. Courtesy Virginia Quintana.

Figure: Left to right. Silviano Lucero, Conferina Lucero Quintana. Courtesy Virginia Quintana.

Papito's Will:

A qienes Concierna   Tecoletite New Mex.
                                      Abril, 24 de 1941

Mis herederos son los siguientes;

Telesfer Lucero
Jesus Lucero
Silviano Lucero
Juan Lucero
Rumaldo Lucero
Ceferina Quintana
Demecio Lucero
Andres B. Lucero

    Mis bienes los cuales deseo repartir al tiempo de morir yo, son los siguientes;

Mis ebejas las cuales a la presente son _____ quiero repartirlas de la manera siguiente;
    EL NUMERO DE OVEJAS que hayga al tiempo de morir yo, es mi voluntad que se repartan entre mis ocho herederos ya mencionados en preporciones iguales para cada uno de ellos.

    A la precente tengo _____ numero de cabras y las cuales deseo que al tiempo de morir yo sean repartidas de la manera siguiente;
CADA UNO DE MIS OCHO HEREDEROS es mi voluntad que reciban su parte en preporciones iguales.

    A la precente tengo el siguiente numero de vacas, las cuales deseo sean repartidas de el siguiente modo;
    TENGO A LA PRESENTE SOLO TRES VACAS las cuales es mi voluntad que al llegarse el tiempo devido sean repartidas en iguales preporciones entre mis herederos ya mencionados. Es entendido que cada uno de ellos tiene y tocara igualmente de el valor de dichos animales.

    MI PROPIEDAD RAIZ ES LA SIGUIENTE
    Terreno de pastos;,   620
son mas o menos 200 acres los cuales deseo y es mi voluntad que al tiempo devido sean repartidos en yguales partes entre mis ocho herederos lla mencionados

    Terreno de riego es el siguiente; el cual esta en el ancon de el Tecoletite. y el cual es 9 acres mas o menos y el cual es mi voluntad que sea repartido en partes iguales entre mis ocho herederos ya mencionados. Dicho terreno de ser repartido despues de morir yo y en niguna manera antes de ese tiempo.

    Ademas tengo tres caballos y un carro el valor de el cual es mi voluntad que al tiempo de morir yo sea repartido igualmente entre mis ocho herederos.

    Ademas es mi voluntady por esta pongo la responsabilidad de dirijir y ver de mis propiedades tanto propiedad RAIZ como propiedad personal en Telesfor lucero y Demecio Lucero quienes haran mis veces en manejar y ver de mis negocios qienes receviran el pago siguiente y de la manera siguiente a saber;

Continuacion de el apunte para hacer el TESTAMENTO de Andres A Lucero
-2-

ADEMAS ES MI ORDEN Y MI VOLUNTAD que al tiempo de morir yo, nada de mi propiedad sera repartida entre mis herederos asta el tanto de que todas mis deudas haygan sido debidamente pagadas a mis acredores, si en caso en ese tiempo hubiera tales deudas.

Certifico que el contenido en el apunte antecedente y el cual incluye dos pajinas es lo que es mi voluntad que sea puesto en mi testamento el cual es mi voluntad que este apunte sea presentado ante un Notario Publico y mi testamento sea echo en conformidad con este apunte.

firmado *Andres † A Lucero*

Testigos *Frank Lucero*
Rumaldo Lucero
Dencisio Lucero

Figure: Will of Andres Lucero. Courtesy of Leroy Duran.

Don Telesfor Lucero:

Figure: Left to right standing Telesfor Lucero, Carlos Paiz, sitting Melecia Garcia [Nov. 28, 1911. Daughter of J. G. Garcia and Bonafacia Lucero from Cañon. [Libro de Partidas de Casamientos, La Iglesia de Antón Chico 1857- 1940]. Abelina Lucero.

Figure: Left to right. Rosa Baca Olguin, Bonifacia Lucero Garcia [grandma Facia], Isabel Baca Bachicha, Melecia Baca Gallegos. Courtesy Betty Olguin. Parents [Bonifacia Lucero Garcia born 1877 and J. In. Garcia].

Rubel:

True farmer

Rubel Lucero farms his land with a used tractor he purchased with the aid of the Division of Vocational Rehabilitation. The tractor needed a complete overhaul but otherwise was not modified to allow him to operate it with one leg. He prefers to operate the tractor without his artificial leg which he says just gets in the way.

Source: Las Optic Aug. 1975.

Family operation

Farming in Tecolotito is a family operation for the Luceros. Lucero's three sons Edward (left), Telesfor (right) and Junior (kneeling) and his wife Elvira all pitch in to run the farm. His son Leo lives in Colorado where he works and attends Colorado State University, and his daughter Sylvia is married and living near the farm.

Source: Las Vegas Optic Aug. 1975.

Don Juanito Lucero:

Figure: Left to Right. Unidentified, Placido Lucero and brother Juan P. Lucero.

August 18, 1905. Placido Lucero from Tecolotito, son of Andres Lucero and Petra Chavez with Sofia Baca, from Chupainas dau. of Leandro Baca and Reyes Morales. [Libro de Partidos de Casamientos, La Iglesia de Anton Chico 1857 to 1940].

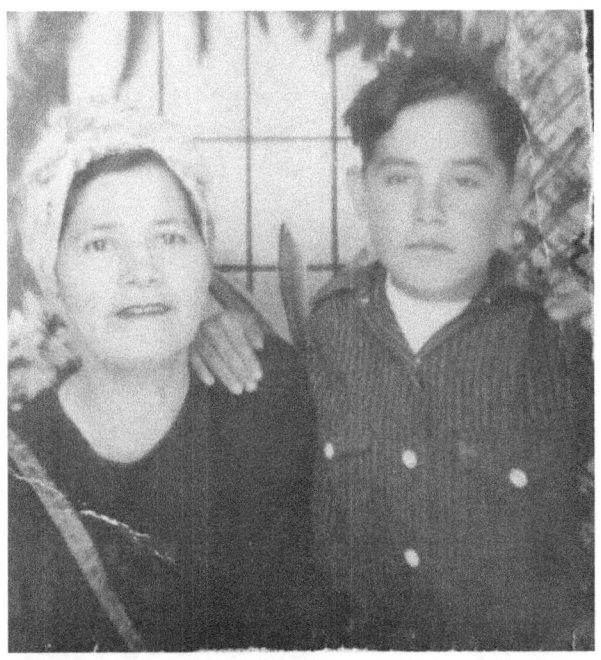

Figure: Left to Right. Rosa Baca Lucero, Alberto Lucero.

Figure: Left to Right. Alvirez Martinez [brother to Graviel], Maria Lucero, Groom, Lala. [Maria the daughter of Queta and Tio Alberto Lucero].

Figure: Rose Lucero 1965 [dau. of Alberto Lucero and Queta].

Figure: José Lucero, Yolanda Lucero. Courtesy Eileen Lucero   *Figure: José Lucero, Alfredo Lucero.*

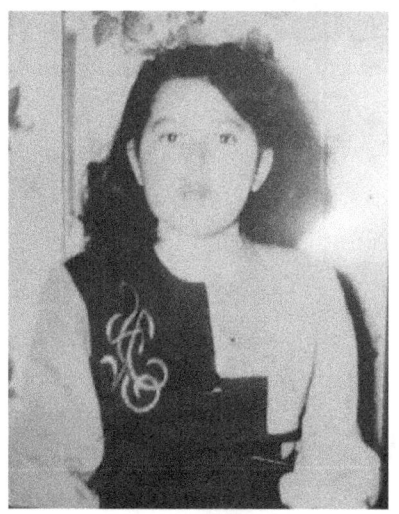

Figure: Petra Patsy Lucero Lerma. Courtesy Jim Chavez.   *Figure: Rita Lucero Hinostroza. Courtesy Juanita Everett Donelson.*

Figure: Left to right. Benerito Lucero, Manuel Lerma.   *Figure: Connie Sandoval Lucero. Courtesy Anna Lucero.*

Figure: Left to right. Connie Sandoval Lucero, Juan P. Lucero, Emilia Lucero. Courtesy Anna Lucero.

Figure: Agneda Olguin Lucero, Alfredo Lucero. Courtesy Anna Lucero.

Figure: Left to right. Juan Lucero Jr., David Lucero, Rosa Baca Lucero, and Violinda Castillo Lucero. Courtesy Josephine Jaramillo.

Figure: Left to right. Front unidentified, Juan Lucero Jr., unidentified. Camp Luna Leather Class. Courtesy: Diana Gonzales.

Figure: Left to right. Back Unidentified, Pete Mares, Juan Lucero Jr., Juan Tenorio Sr., Prospero Pino, Unidentified, Unidentified, Moises Sanchez, Unidentified. Front Spouses Louisa Tenorio, Unidentified, Bella Pino, Violinda Lucero, Unidentified, Unidentified. School Bus Drivers and spouses from SRCS.

The first feeder bus route from Tecolotito to Anton Chico was in 1964. Juan Lucero Jr. [my father] drove a red and white 1965 Mercury [car].

Grace Tenorio Urioste and Rose Lucero were some of the bussed students. Prospero Pino the bus driver in Anton Chico picked the Tecolotito students and drove them to SRCS. The following year my father started driving a new 1965 International Bus with an approximate 9 passenger capacity to Santa Rosa.

Figure: Left to Right. Vicente Jaramillo and Juan Pablo Lucero.

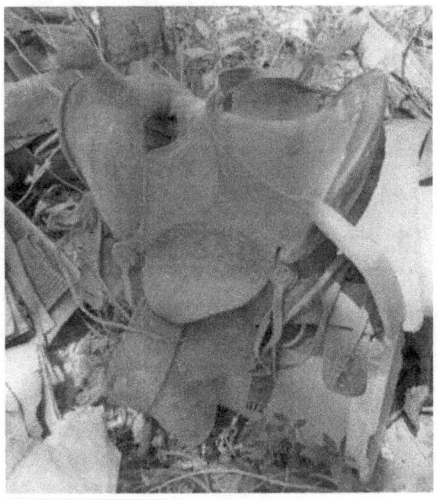

Figure: Juan P. Lucero old high back saddle. Courtesy of Joe Romero.

Grandpa Juan's saddle was sold to Freddie Martinez by Uncle Fred Lucero. Then sold to Jose Eufemio Romero for $75.00. [Jose Eufemio Romero, personal communication].

Figure: unidentified. Courtesy of Sylvia Lucero [Bobo] and Adriana Lucero Archuleta.

Las Escardas:

Figure: Left to Right. Mike Valdez, Melesia [Molly] Lucero Valdez. Cotton fields in Texas 50 years ago. Courtesy Mike Valdez.

The way of life for most of us in Tecolotito was migrating to Muleshoe, Littlefield, Morton, Hereford, Needmore, Circleback, Stegall, or West camp to work on the cottonfields in Texas.

Hoeing the huge cottonfields was the summer work. This was the yearly migration for the Lucero's, Tenorio's, and many other families from Tecolotito for the summer months. The trip required some limited packing of essentials.

Our mother's packed cotton filled mattresses which they rolled up tightly after washing the outer covers and airing out and pulling the cotton apart. Finally stuffing the mattress cover and tying the inner strings and rolling it tightly.

A few dishes and utensils were put in the cajete [tub] along with flour, salt, sugar, and other basic food. On the sidestep of the old 1949 Chevy was the old, galvanized milk container wrapped with gunny sacks then tied down and filled with water. The gunny sacks were then wet to keep the water cool. And on the passenger side mirror was the canvass canteen full of fresh cool water. Water was important since it was summer work, and everyone would be drinking a lot.

The clothing packed for the field work was pants and a long sleeve shirt to protect us from the sun. Gloves were worn by some of the migrants. But the most important tool was the hoe. One for each family member and the extra hoe in case one broke. A file was also taken for sharpening the hoes every afternoon.

A straw hat was worn by the men and some of the children. Most of the women made their own papalinas [bonnets].

Papalinas:

Making papalinas [bonnets] was done prior to going to the escardas. Working in the sun required protection to the head from the sun. The papalina was made with hard material strips of about 2 inches by 12 inches long from Tide soap boxes. About 6 strips were needed. The flour sacks made good papalina material as the outer lining. Two pieces of 12- inches by 12- inch material for the top of the papalina then sewn together and leaving the 2- inch sections to insert all 6 strips. The shade around the ears was a strip of 2 inches by 24 inches that was sewn around the square of Tide strips. On the back of the head was a half- moon shaped piece of material the size of square strips made for the back of head and sewn. Finally, the 24- inch strip was sewn along the square for the ears and back of the head. Pleating some of the material as needed. Two strands were made to tie the papalina under the chin in place.

Packing for the trip was done the day before leaving. Most families planned and migrated to Texas in May after school ended. It was a very early start the next morning for the all- day trip. Some families travelled on different trucks and some rode together. A canvass had been put over the varandal [bed rack] of the truck for protection of wind, sun, or any elements. Children or adults rode on the back of the old trucks.

The trip was slow at about 50 mph or slower and hoping that no flats on the old tires with tubes that had many cold patches already. And or over heating of the old 6- cylinder trucks. Reaching Santa Rosa meant stopping at Square Deal to buy bologna, bread, and soda.

The next stop was at Cañada de Juan de Dios to eat lunch under the nice shade of the old Alamo. The stop was a good break for everyone. Travelling the rest of the afternoon until reaching the destination in Texas. Getting to the barracks late Saturday afternoon and unpacking quickly because work would begin Monday.

Late Sunday afternoon the mayordomo [foreman] Juan Tenorio talked to the patron [boss]. Deciding for the first day of work. The patron had a list of the farmers and took the mayordomo and my dad to show them the cotton field to begin at 7 o'clock the next morning to 5 o'clock in the afternoon with a 30-minute lunch. Working for 10 hours a day. Saturday was half a day of work. The mayordomo contracted all the adults at .60 cents an hour per person.

Babysitting:

Babysitting was hard for a seven- or eight-year-old little girl. Staying in the back of the truck during the hot days was difficult. And when Sami, my baby brother started crying, I could change the diaper but then if he was hungry there was nothing, I could do about it because he was breast fed by mom. Hoping for mom to come to the truck quickly. But it was so much waiting in the endless and long cotton fields.

In desperation I yelled out to the workers in the field, "quien quiere darle chiche al Sami"? Tio Arcenio's daughter Fabiola yelled back, "yo"! But Fabiola was only responding to the desperation of a little girl and a crying baby. However, Fabiola's response gave me hope until mom got to the truck.

I finally got to work at nine years old, something I really wanted to do. Earning .50 cents an hour and interacting with the family. My job had been to babysit.

Towards the end of the escardas our mothers oversaw the savings. By now Juan and my dad asked, "trae's tu bolsita Louisa"? And laughed jokingly! The bolsita [purse] was a sock and safety pin attached to the bra.

Chile:

The excitement of returning home to New Mexico built up after spending the summer working in the fields. My mother got excited because she knew that chile would be in season once we got to New Mexico. Buying chile immediately from anyone selling a bucket for .60 cents in the old town bridge in Las Vegas from Anton Chico, Sena, Dilia, or El Cerrito. My father also bought chile from his friend Don Luis Saiz in Puerto De Luna. Once school started and driving the bus to Santa Rosa gave him a chance to buy chile from his friend. Although Puerto De Luna Chile was small, but it was tasty!

Preparing the chile was a process that began over the hot wood stove. Flipping and roasting all sides of every chile and then laying the chiles on a wet cloth towel. Once the chile cooled off the peeling, pulling off the stem and scraping off the seeds could begin. Hopefully all of the chile was picked when it was ripe, and the seeds were not black since that would cause a stomachache. My mom didn't scrape off the seeds though. Finally, the chile would be put into a bowl and mom would squish it with her hand until it was well done then she added the garlic.

Year after year during the summer months we worked in the cotton fields. The work was hard, but we learned the hardships of physical labor and work ethics.

Don Rumaldo Lucero:

Figure: Rumaldo Lucero Sr. Standing, Feliciana Esquibel Lucero [Tia Chana] sitting, Merejildo [boy], baby unidentified. Courtesy Leroy Duran.

Figure: Left to right. Cordy, Feliciana Esquibel Lucero, Rumaldo Jr. Lucero.

Figure: Left to right. Ernie Lucero, Andrea Lucero, tío Rumaldo Lucero, Rosa Lucero Ortiz. Courtesy Leroy Duran.

Figure: Left to right. Rumaldo Lucero sitting, Eddie Lucero sitting and Ernie Lucero standing. Cotton fields in Texas. Courtesy Leroy Duran.

Tio Rumaldo Lucero on his new Ford in Texas.

Melesia:

Figure: Melesia Lucero Valdez born 4/29/1928, Miguel [Mike] Valdez. Courtesy of Mike Valdez.

Figure: Left to Right. Rumaldo Lucero Jr., Miguel [Mike] Valdez. Courtesy Mike Valdez

Figure: Left to Right. Mike Valdez, Melesia [Molly] Lucero Valdez. Cotton fields in Texas 50 years ago. Courtesy Mike Valdez.

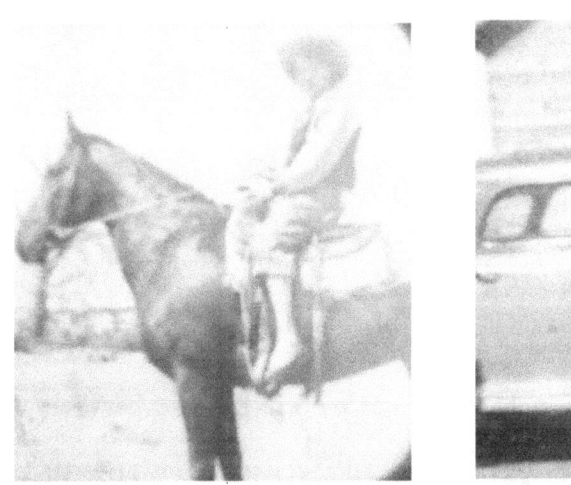 

Figure: Estella Lucero DeLeon. Courtesy Elizabeth Torres. Figure: Estella Lucero. Courtesy Elizabeth Torres Rodriguez.

Figure: Left to right. Theresa, Pete Lucero with Pauline, and Rosemary. Boy unidentified girl unidentified. Courtesy Elizabeth Torres Rodriguez.

Veneranda:

Figure: Veneranda Lucero Duran. Courtesy Leroy Duran.

Veneranda was born 10/17/1937 in Tecolotito, N. M. to Rumaldo Lucero and Feliciana Esquibel Lucero and baptized by Ascencion Encinias and Felipita Garcia.

Veneranda was middle of eleven children. She learned to drive by pulling a work trailer while helping her family as a migrant. Veneranda rode horse back which was part of life and transportation.

Veneranda's parents Rumaldo and Feliciana left the children and travelled to Las Vegas, N.M. by horse and wagon for "Segamos y recogemos" [follow and pick up] to buy needed goods.

Jesse and Veneranda:

Veneranda during the migration to Texas met Jesse in Littlefield at a carnival and made continuous weekend dance dates. Of course her brother's Steve and Eddie were not happy with the courting. The two brothers picked fights on poor Jesse.

The dates continued with a lunch date at Curly Tops Drive Inn. Placing an order for food when you're young and short of money is a problema. The menu with coney dogs was more affordable for Jesse but when he got to the car Veneranda knew what she wanted. She wanted a Burger and not a coney dog. Jesse had to return to buy a Burger at the counter and no money was left in his pocket.

Veneranda's family migrated on to Colorado to farm and of course Jesse followed.

And by 11/10/1956 there was a wedding in Littlefield, Texas. Jesse Jr. was born in Littlefield. Then moving on to O'Donnell in 1958 by the Ford dealer. DOT and MJ were born in O'Donnell. Jesse was a mechanic now and got the chance to work on Dan Blocker's [Hoss Cartwright from Bonanza] car.

By 1960 Veneranda cleaned house while Jesse farmed for Mr. Myatt. Leroy and Sandra were then born in Abernathy.

There home was a 1 bedroom 1 bath house. By now grandma Chana, Uncle Ernie, and Aunt Rose lived behind the house in a Little barrack.

Jesse went to farm with Dean Mcguire for more money and a 2 bedroom house. Veneranda watched the young children and babysat the McGuire kids too. Her knowledge of sewing, mending, ironing, and embroidering doilies was another way of making extra money. She sold and sewed or ironed for the ladies in town. Veneranda altered the childrens clothes and would add ruffles to the bottom of the jeans as they grew.

Veneranda often wore big rollers and covered them with a headscarf. Meantime wearing a housecoat.

During her pregnancy with Tammy her youngest, she and the children sat outside and ate cucumbers and lemon juice.

The children had chores which was collecting eggs from the chicken coop. Leroy was scared of the chickens and Sandra was the one going into the coop. After all Leroy made her go in. The other animals were Henrietta the rooster and a pig acting like Dandy the dog.

Those were the days when Jesse coached baseball for the boys after all he had played in Lubbock with the "Hubbers". Dorothy kept books and Sandra got bubblegum for the team. But on Wednesday night Jesse made the outing "Wrestling" an event for the kids. It included .5 cent popcorn! Veneranda was pretty mad about that activity.

A special holiday meant taking the girls shopping for dresses at Levines in Lubbock.

Finally, getting a job with Texas Tech where she retired. Receiving several awards and recognition during her tenure and a letter of Recognition from the Dean. Loving her Tech-ity Tech! **But above all telling her six children and grandchildren how proud she was of her "Lucero" heritage and reminding them,**

"be proud you are Lucero". [Leroy Duran, personal communication, Nov. 10, 2020].

Figure: Veneranda Lucero Duran, Jesse Duran wedding. Courtesy Leroy Duran.

Andrea:

Figure: Celestino Gonzales and Andrea Lucero Gonzales. Courtesy Victor Gonzales.

Figure: Celestino Gonzales. Courtesy Nick Gonzales.

Andrea Lucero Gonzales married into a family that has served and continues to serve the U.S. Military service with over 150 years. A tradition started by Ruperto Gonzales.

Figure: Left to right. Daniel Gonzales, Alex Gonzales, Nick Gonzales, Victor Gonzales, and Celestino Gonzales. Courtesy Nick Gonzales.

All in the family
The Gonzáles: 100 years of Army service

By Master Sgt. C.S. Allbright
Fifth U.S. Army PAO

Despite its appearance as a simple promotion ceremony, an event that took place last February in Texas represented one American family's tradition of 100 years of combined service to the nation spanning across three generations.

Nick C. Gonzáles, 39, was promoted to lieutenant colonel at Fifth U.S. Army Headquarters, Fort Sam Houston, carrying forward a legacy of service. He's currently the plans and policy chief for G-3 Training, Fifth Army.

Pinning on his new rank insignia was his wife, Regina. Also his father, Celestino Gonzáles, a retired Army sergeant major and decorated Vietnam War veteran. The spirit of the newly promoted officer's grandfather was also in the room. The late Ruperto "Bob" Gonzáles started the family's military tradition during World War II.

Bob Gonzáles joined the Army in 1943 from San Jon, a small farming community in eastern New Mexico, serving in the Aleutian Islands during the war. He completed his service in 1947. Five of Bob Gonzáles' six sons served in the Army. "He started the tradition, my father continued the fine tradition and now I'm carrying it on," said Lt. Col. Gonzáles. "My grandfather was very patriotic. He always preached the need to support and defend the country. He'd say we have a great country, and we must do everything to protect it," he added.

With his father and uncles in the Army, Gonzáles was raised surrounded by the backdrop of military communities at Fort Bragg, N.C., Germany, and Okinawa. "Being born a military brat, it was almost ingrained in us. I can remember being a young kid —3 or 4 years old— and we were running around playing army, he said. "It grew in our blood."

As far as Celestino Gonzáles is concerned, he served in the Army from 1956 through 1986, including two tours in Vietnam as an infantryman. The airborne, air-assault qualified soldier and recipient of the Combat Infantryman's Badge received two Bronze Stars and other decorations for his service before retiring as a sergeant major. His final assignment was with the Reserve Officer Training Corps at Eastern New Mexico University in Portales, N.M.

Moving "home" to New Mexico was good for Celestino and Maria Gonzáles and their seven children. All of their children, four boys and three girls, attended the university, and the four boys either served or are currently serving in the Army: Victor, 41, is in the Texas Army National Guard, and recently completed a year at Fort Sam Houston supporting Homeland Security efforts; Daniel, 29, is with the Army Reserve in Ogden, Utah. He was deployed for the 2002 Winter Olympics and recently came off active-duty status; Alex, 24, is an active duty, ordenance second lieutenant at First U.S. Cavalry Division at Fort Hood.

It was at Alex's commissioning, officiated by his brother Nick, that the Gonzáles family totaled up the number of years of Army service. Starting with Ruperto and his sons, and then Celestino and his sons, the number was well over 100 years.

The girls—Theresa and Tina, third and fourth oldest; and Veronica, the sixth child—are also closely tied to the military. Theresa's husband served in the Air Force and is a Gulf War veteran. Veronica's husband is a CPT in the Army Reserve. Siblings Daniel, Alex and Tina were among the family members and friends in attendance at their brother promotion ceremony. "This is a memory that will last forever. It gives me and our entire family a sense of pride," Daniel Gonzáles said on that occasion.

Even though the Army way was dominant in the Gonzáles family, young Nick gave few indicators about his future military aspirations, his father said.

"When he was very young and had long hair, Nick bought a motorcycle with the money he earned mowing yards." Actually, the first real indication that Nick was serious about going Army was when he enrolled in the ROTC program during his college years.

It was in 1985, after attending Eastern New Mexico University, that Nick Gonzáles received his Army commission as an armored cavalry officer. Like his father and two of his brothers, he's airborne qualified. After serving as a tank platoon leader, Gonzáles switched to the quartermaster branch. He also served as a liaison officer with the Navy during the war in Kosovo. "I have had a unique career," he said. One of the most rewarding events of his career involved his service in Kosovo, from June 1998 through July 1999. After the Kosovo air war was ramping down he was involved in designing

Source: Vista Magazine, p. 18, June 2003. Courtesy Nick Gonzales.

Figure: Left to right President George W. Bush 43rd President and Nick Gonzales. Courtesy Nick Gonzales.

Figure: Left to right back row [Framed Picture of Celestino Gonzales], Victor Gonzales, Nick Gonzales, Nick Gamez, Erica Gonzales [Daughter of Nick Gonzales], Daniel Gonzales, and Alex Gonzales. Courtesy Nick Gonzales.

Rose:

Figure: Rosa Lucero Ortiz and John T. Ortiz [from Las Vegas, N.M.] wedding. Courtesy Rosa Lucero Ortiz.

Ernie:

Figure: Ernie Lucero. Courtesy Phyllis Lewis Burton.

The Ax:

Ernie, the youngest of Tio Rumaldo's children helped by bringing water from the acequia. The big sandstone wheel was under the big cotton wood trees by the acequia and was used to sharpen the ax. The boxed bottom of the sandstone wheel needed water when being turned with the foot paddle to sharpen the ax which made it easier to cut wood.

This time Ernie wanted to play with the neighbor's kids, but Tio Rumaldo sternly said, "no, trae agua de la acequia". Ernie had to fill the box with water and then turn the paddle while Tio Rumaldo held the ax blade on the sandstone wheel. Work and chores needed to be done.

Figure: Left to right back row. Melecia, Flavio, Rumaldo Jr., Estella, Veneranda, Esteban. Front Eduardo, Andrea, Rosa, Ernesto. Courtesy Elizabeth Torres Rodriguez.

Don Demecio Lucero:

Figure: Left to Right.standing. Melaquias Tenorio, Sinforosa [Sinforiana] Ortega Tenorio. Sitting Demecio Lucero and Manuelita Salas Lucero wedding 8-8-1927. Courtesy of Leroy Duran.

Cipio Salas y Esposa

y

Andres A. Lucero y Esposa

Participan la presencia de usted y su apreciable familia al enlace conyugal de sus hijos

Manuelita Salas

y

Demecio Lucero

Que se celebrará en la parroquia de Anton Chico en Anton Chico, N. M., el día, 8 de Agosto de 1927 a las 8:30 a. m., y en seguida a una recepción en casa de los primeros en El Tecolotito y por la noche a un baile en la zala de don Rumaldo Castillo.

Figure: Wedding Invitation for Manuelita Salas and Demecio Lucero. Courtesy Leroy Duran.

Demecio Jr:

Figure: Left to right. Candida Aragon Lucero, Leroy Duran, Demecio Lucero Jr. Courtesy Leroy Duran.

El Ojito en El Apache:

Demecio Jr. at the age of 8 years old received a yearly call from his grandpa Escipio Salas during the summer rains. The rain usually washed weeds and tree branches into the ojito [spring] the water source was on the east of highway 84 and was used at the Apache ranch which is west of the highway.

The ojito was about 6 feet deep with clear water and had a pipe to allow the water to flow out and create a pond and then water flowed across the road to provide water for the ranch. At the top of the pipe was a screen with a wire tied around it to allow water to flow freely but the screen needed to be removed and cleaned and then put back securely.

Demecio Jr. had a job with his grandpa Escipio which meant a possible horse ride from Tecolotito to El Apache. The payment of $5.00 back in those days was a lot of money. The task was to dive down and remove the screen and then take the second dive to replace and tie the screen. Uncle Daniel or the other uncles never volunteered to do the job, but it was an easy $5.00 for an eight-year-old that liked been in water!

Figure: James Abercrombie, store in Anton Chico. Courtesy Leroy Duran.

Figure: Abercrombie, store in Anton Chico

Sons of Manuel Lucero Sr.:

Figure: Cristobal Lucero [son of Manuel Lucero and Relles Sandoval Lucero]. Courtesy Diana Tenorio Gonzales.

Source: Ancestry Cristobal Lucero. New Mexico, U.S., WWI Records, 1917-1919.

Figure: Gregorio Lucero born 8/26/1890 [son of Manuel Lucero and Relles Sandoval Lucero].

Source: Ancestry Gregorio Lucero. New Mexico, U.S., WWI Records, 1917-1919.

Doña Aurelia:

Figure: Left to right. Aurelia Lucero Marquez and brother Pedro [Petro] Lucero. Courtesy Leroy Duran.

Aurelia Lucero Marquez is the daughter of Benigno Lucero and Victoria Baca. Aurelia's siblings were Maria Relles born in 1879, Estolano born 1880, Emilio born 1882, Sostenes born 1883, Maria de los Reyes born 1885, Roman born 1887, Delfida born 1890, Veneranda born 1891, Maria Rumalda born 1893, Balbina born 1895, Francisca born 1897, Pedro Jose born 1899, Maria Aurelia born 1900, Juan Jose born 1903, Maria Gregoria born 1905, Lucinda born 1907. [Sources Anton Chico St. Joseph's Catholic records] and 1910 Census.

Aurelia Lucero Marquez was the granddaughter of Roman Lucero and Maria Rumalda Sandoval, my grandfather Juan Lucero's grandparents also.

Christmas Holidays:

During the Christmas holidays Tia Aurelia was the best place to go to. On Christmas Eve [en los oremos] going out late in the afternoon was the tradition and of course all the village children were out going from house to house. Most families had already put up their piñon Christmas trees. The decorations were mostly colored bulbs and some cotton and a tin foil star at the top of the tree.

Children yelled out when approaching the doorway of the neighbor's house. Yelling out, "Mis oremos Angelitos semos[somos] del cielo vinimos a pedir oremos". "Si no me dan oremos puertas y ventanas quebraremos". Going to all the houses was extremely hard, especially if there was snow or freezing cold. Tia Aurelia always had a big box with peanuts and hard candy. Aurelia dug into her box with her big hand and scooped out a hand full of candy. The children carried a little bag.

My sister Benigna was always happy to see her Madrina Aurelia because she always had a gift under the tree. All the neighborhood kids made a stop at her house. Jerry Tenorio also got excited because he knew that his Madrina Aurelia had a gift for him. The children were all happy to see their bags filled up. Tio Pedro also enjoyed the children and joked around with them. He asked, "que vinieron a rezar"? [did you come to pray"?]

On New Year's Day we all went out early in the morning again. From house to house in the cold and yelling out the traditional "Mis Años Nuevos". By the time that we went around the village our hands and feet were freezing, and our noses were red and running. The hardships of going throughout the community was an all-morning walk. The goodies that were collected in the bag were hard candy, saltine crackers, and even a slice of apple pie which didn't mix quite well in the bags.

Doña Margarita had us sing and then kneel and say a prayer before giving us saltines. And that wasn't the expected or desired treat.

Sunday Church:

Tío Pedro Marquez drove tía Aurelia to Church in Anton Chico every Sunday. He drove his dark green 1940's Chevrolet pickup. Tía Aurelia got down and attended the services. But tío Pedro sat on his pickup smoking his pipe and waited for tía Aurelia until she got out of church.

Leña:

Tío Pedro and tía Aurelia got leña on their 1940's green Chevrolet pickup. Again, tío Pedro drove tía Aurelia. This time to the monte [Mountains] to get leña.

Tía Aurelia got down the truck and chopped the wood and then she loaded it. In the meantime, tío Pedro sat on the truck smoking his pipe.

Don Pedro Lucero:

Figure: Pedro Lucero, Louisa Gonzales Lucero. Courtesy Tina Lucero Aragón.

Libro de Partidas de Casamientos, La Iglesia de Anton Chico 1857 to 1940

April 16, 1930. **Pedro Lucero**, from Anton Chico, son of José I. Lucero and Maria Sandoval born in Anton Chico, with **Luisa Gonzáles** from and born in Anton Chico, dau of Em. Gonzáles and Juana Chávez.

Source: New Mexico Marriages Anton Chico La Iglesia de San Jose April 1857- December 1940.

Jose Ines was born 4-23-1851 the son of Roman Lucero and Maria Rumalda Sandoval. Maria Sandoval dau. of José Ignacio Sandoval and Maria Antonia Martin.

Figure: Alfonso Aragon, Tina Aragon. Courtesy Tina Lucero Aragon.

Figure: Left to right. Christine Quintana Aragon, Alfonso Aragon, Lee Aragon. Courtesy Tina Lucero Aragon.

Figure: Alfonso Aragon, Tina Lucero Aragon [NMHU Bachelor's degree]. Courtesy Tina Lucero Aragon.

Don Merejildo Esquibel:

Figure: Left to right. Merejildo Esquibel [Born 1863]. Married 12-24-1897 to Juana Maria Salas [Born 5-6-1863]. Woman unidentified. Feliciana Esquibel Lucero [little girl tía Chana]. Courtesy Leroy Duran.

Mayo 10 de 1863. En Antón Chico, bautize a Juana María Salas, nacida el 6 del mismo mez, hija legitima de Andrés Salas y de Feliciana Lucero. Padrinos: Jesús María Lucero y Prudencio Martínez. Source: Sacramental Records from the Archives of the Santa Fe, New Mexico Baptisms Antón Chico, La Yglesia de San José 1857-1897 pg. 466.

Figure: Merejildo Esquibel and Juana Maria Salas. Married 12-24-1897 age 34 [2nd marriage]. Courtesy Leroy Duran.

Figure: Left to right. Unidentified, Feliciana Esquibel Lucero, Rumaldo Lucero. Courtesy Leroy Duran.

Figure: Left to right. Feliciana Esquibel Lucero, girl unidentified. Courtesy Leroy Duran.

Tía Feliciana Esquibel Lucero in Muleshoe, Texas. A celebration of First Communion at Immaculate Conception with Jose and Flora Baca. Tia Chana was the sponsor of the daughter of Jose and Flora Baca.

Figure: Left to right. Petra Quintana, Rumaldo Lucero, Isabel Quintana [las cuatas]. Courtesy of Leroy Duran.

Mr. and Mrs. Duran (1956)

Figure: Left to right. Jesse Duran, Veneranda Lucero Duran. Courtesy Leroy Duran.

Lugarda Lucero:

Figure: Left to Right. Lugarda Lucero Martinez [mom], Corina, Louisa, William, Manuel [dad]. Courtesy William Martinez.

Lugarda Lucero Martinez daughter of Andres Lucero and Corina Gonzales Lucero.

Figure: William Martinez SP 4 in Berlin, Germany 1986-89. Courtesy William Martinez.

William Martinez a graduate of Robertson in Las Vegas, N.M. immediately went for Basic Training and AIT in July-Oct. of 1982 at Fort Benning Georgia. Then left for Korea and spent 13 months there 3 months at DMZ patrols, recons, night ambushes, quick reaction platoon and 1- month guard collier. Although in infantry an MP Arm Band was worn and earned an IMJIN scouts award and 1st Army Achievement Metal.

William then spent 3 years at Fort Lewis, Washington from 1983-86 and then got his first honorable discharge. Minutes later re-enlisted for 4 more years. Serving 3 years in Berlin Brigade in West Germany before the wall came down.

Orders then came to Fort Knox, Kentucky. Finally got out in July 1990.

Figure: William Martinez.   Figure: Left to right. Manuel Martinez, William, Lugarda Lucero Martinez. Courtesy William Martinez.

Figure: Service Patches. Courtesy William Martinez.

Don Leo Baca:

Figure: Left to Right. Monica Gutierrez Hines, Leopoldo Baca, Josephine Gutierrez Roybal. Courtesy of Josephine Roybal.

Figure: Merlinda Gutierrez Salazar. Courtesy Josephine Roybal.

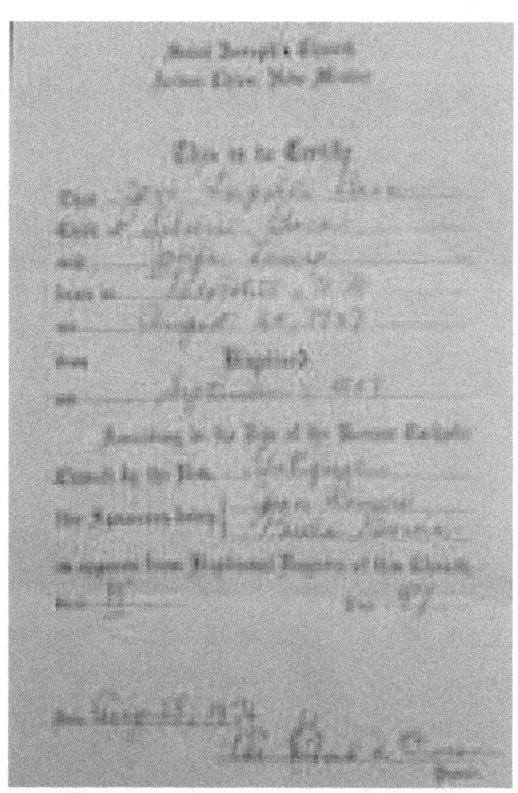

Source: Baptismal Certificate Leopoldo Baca. Courtesy Joe Lee Baca.

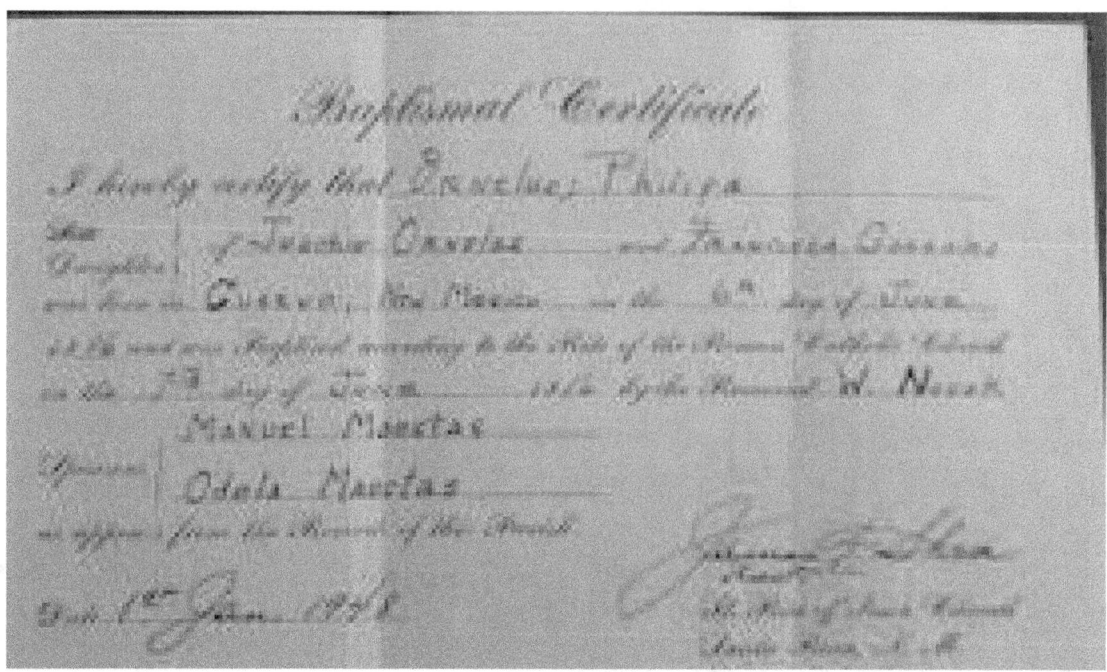

Source: Baptismal Certificate Philipa Ornelas. Courtesy Joe Lee Baca.

Tia Pita:

Philipa Ornelas Baca, known as Pita, was born at El Cuervo, N. Mex. in 1916. Her father was Joaquin Ornelas. Pita's mother Francisca passed away when she was a baby. Pita had an older sister Ignacia and two older half-brothers.

Pita and her older sister had a hard life and were very poor. Her father liked to drink, and survival was now all about hard work for Pita. Joaquin, Ignacia, and Pita travelled to the escobas [broomfields] and cottonfields at a young age. Migration to Southeastern N.Mex. and Western Texas was by horse drawn wagon. As Pita grew into a young woman, she would keep up with the men or outwork the men in theatre group. Her work ethics were outstanding.

Marriage

Pita's first marriage was to William Hern, the brother of Roberto, Nick, and Juan Hern. Pita later married Leopoldo Baca after the passing of William Hern.

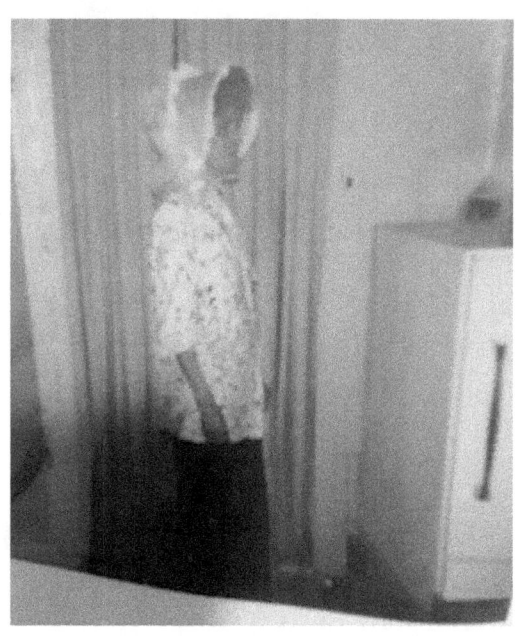

Figure: Pita Baca. Courtesy Joe Lee Baca.

Creativity:

Pita was a very creative person. Here she is modeling a papalina [bonnet]. The papalina was made with cardboard for the visor usually from a box of tide. This stiff part of the papalina created a good visor. The back was a poofed piece of material when sewn up. And a neck pleated piece of material and then the ties. The material was usually a flowery print material and finally a white lace trim.

Crocheting mantelitos [crocheted table covers] and handmade colchas [blankets] were part of Tia Pita's projects that she enjoyed making.

Figure: Left to Right. Guadalupe Montaño Baca, Joe Lee Baca, Pita Baca. Courtesy Joe Lee Baca.

Tienditas:

Tío Leo and Tia Pita had a tiendita at the abuelita Josefita Baca residence in south Tecolotito. They later moved up to the old School house in Tecolotito and transformed it into a store in which Leo and Pita sold groceries, clothing, shoes, and gas.

Tio Leo bought the Jose Encinias home in Anton Chico along with nine angus cows and a bull. The house he remodeled into a second tiendita. Tia Pita and Joe Lee attempted to run the tiendita but it was short lived and later sold to Christian Maestas. The store later became Lillie's Store in Anton Chico.

Culture and food:

Cooking lots of food only to feed visiting family or friends was also learned by tia Pita.

Making Chicos:

The old Tecolotito school house was home for Tia Pita, tío Leo, and Joe Lee. A cisterna [cistern] which was used for the old school became a fire pit for making chicos. Tia Pita instructed Joe Lee and some cousins to make chicos. The first thing was to build the fire and allow it to burn until the red-hot embers emerged. Next was to cover the embers with wet burlap sacks in a few layers thick. Then came the ears of corn in wet burlap sacks and finally covered the corn with more wet burlap sacks. The cistern opening was then covered with a lid and covered with dirt to keep the steam from escaping. The next day out came the sacks of corn and eating corn on the cob was fun. Finally, the corn was hung out on perches to dry for a few days. The corn was then separated from the husk and bagged for use or sale. [Joe Lee Baca, personal communication, May 18, 2020].

Christmas Baggie:

On Christmas day you could expect a specially made baggie full of candy. At Tia Pita's and Leo's country store.

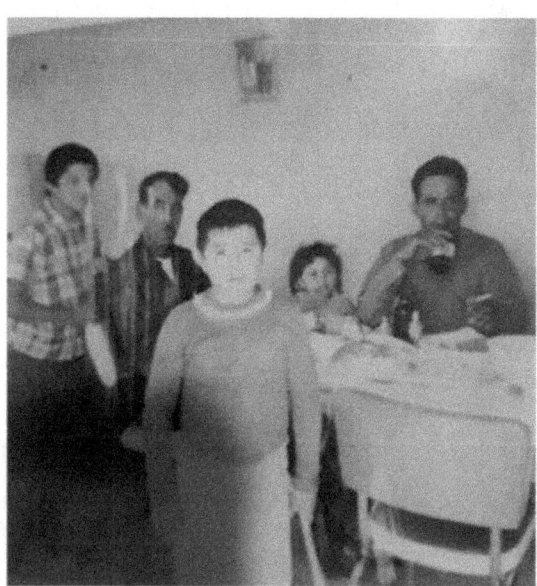

Figure: Left to Right. Junior Lucero, Leo Baca, Josie Lerma, Reynaldo Lerma. Standing Joe Lee Baca. Courtesy of Joe Lee Baca.

Bonifacio Baca:

Figure: Left to right. Anna Pacheco Gomez, Elena Pacheco Baca, Bonifacio Garcia Baca, Amalia Lucero. Courtesy John Baca.

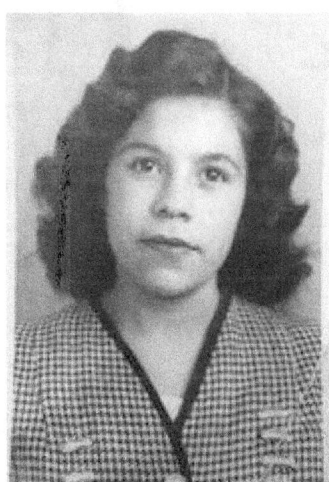

Figure: Bonifacio Baca. Courtesy John Baca.   *Figure: Elena Pacheco Baca. Courtesy John Baca*

Figure: Left to right. Sedelina Paiz Pacheco, Rosalio Pacheco, Elena Pacheco Baca, Bonifacio Baca, Amalia Lucero. Courtesy John Baca.

Figure: Filandro Sandoval Sr. and Merlinda Baca Sandoval. Courtesy Merlinda Baca Sandoval.

Filandro served around thirty years in the Anton Chico Land Grant Board of Trustees. And looked after his cows during retirement.

Don Jose Anastacio Maria Baca:

Family:

Jose Anastacio Baca Born 1832 and his father was Miguel Geronimo Baca and Mother Maria Ramona Ortega born 1837.

Jose Anastacio married Maria Manuela Gutierrez Sept. 11, 1853. Maria's parents Florencio Gutierrez and Magdalena Sanchez.

Civil War:

Great-great grandfather Jose Anastacio Baca was in the Civil War from March 5, 1864, to Oct. 15, 1866. His rank was Sergeant, Company E.

Buffalo Hunt:

J. Baca had been out on a buffalo hunt. Hunts often meant going out of the home for months at a time. There were buffalo at Llano Estacado. The two wheeled caretta was pulled by an ox. It was a time-consuming hunt. Several buffaloes were hunted and processed.

After coming back there was a new baby in the home. Maria Gutierrez is the wife of J. Baca and the mother of a new baby. The baby's name was Silverio, and he was born June 27, 1876. Silverio had blue eyes and J. Baca found this conflicting. It is said that Maria had been impregnated by John Harrison. Cousin John Baca asked his mother on two occasions "where do the blue eyes come from?" He was referring to his dad and family. She responded, "Hito grandma says you should be Harrison and not Baca". John was referring to the Silverio Baca and Maria Manuela Gutierrez Baca family. [John Baca, personal communication].

John Harrison tried to adopt Silverio Baca but never succeeded.

By 1884 John Harrison had been operating a general merchandise store and was a livestock dealer in Anton Chico. The population in Anton Chico was around 1,500. John Harrison later moved to Pecos, N. M. where he owned "The Harrison Country Store". He later sold the Country Store to the Adelo's and moved back to Anton Chico.

Reymundo Harrison, the son of John Harrison too had a general merchandise business in 1903 in Anton Chico.

[F. Stanley, "The Anton Chico Story" 1975].

Figure: Nicolas Baca [brother of Jose Anastacio Maria Baca].

A. Nicolas Baca [his older brother] took charge and looked after Silverio. It is noted in the census that they lived in Encino, N.M.

Great grandfather Silverio Baca married Josefita Lucero and fathered Rosa [my grandma] Hipolito, Silverio, Leopoldo, and Adela. All these children later noticed that they themselves had children or grandchildren with blue eyes along with a light complexion.

Great-great grandmother Maria Manuela Gutierrez at the age of 69 lived in Tecolotito with Great grandfather Silverio Baca and great grandmother Josefita Lucero Baca in 1910. By now Maria Manuela Gutierrez Baca at the age of 69 was blind. [U.S. Census Bureau, Tecolotito 1910].

Tio Leo grandma Rosa's brother continuously told Tio Jose Lucero, the family, and friends that he was supposed to be Harrison and not Baca. I heard the comment also. DNA also shows Irish and British blood lines in the Josefita and Silverio Baca family.

[7-741.]

Page No. __1__
Supervisor's District No. _New Mexico_
Enumeration District No. _56_

Eleventh Census of the United States.

SPECIAL SCHEDULE.

SURVIVING SOLDIERS, SAILORS, AND MARINES, AND WIDOWS, ETC.

Persons who served in the Army, Navy, and Marine Corps of the United States during the war of the rebellion (who are survivors), and widows of such persons, in _San Miguel_, County of _San Miguel_, Territory/State of _New Mexico_, enumerated in June, 1890.   _Arthur Morrison_, Enumerator.

No.	House No. From Schedule No. 1	Family No.	Names of Surviving Soldiers, Sailors, and Marines, and Widows.	Rank	Company	Name of Regiment or Vessel	Date of Enlistment	Date of Discharge	Length of Service (Yrs. Mos. Days)
1	1	1	William L. Hall	Captain	E	1 Rg. Infty Volunteers	July 1, 1861	Aug. 31, 1864	3 5 x
2	1	1	Thomas Stout	Private	E	38 Colo Infty (Artillery Corps)	1863	1866	3 x x
3	5	7	Edward N. Lewis	Private	D	9 Kansas Cav	Oct 1862	Aug 1865	2 10 x
4	7	9	Sharlton Ford	Bugler	H	U.S. Cavalry	1861	1869	10 x x
5	49	52	Midor Torres	Corporal	B	1 N. My. Infty	July 2, 1861	1864	3 1
6	47	50	Florentino Herrera	Private	B	3rd N. Mex. Infty	1864	1867	3 x x
7	64	67	Fernandez Arguello	Private	J	2 N. Mex. Infty	1865	1866	3 x x
8	71	74	Ramon Lucero	Private	G	1 N. Mex. Cav Vol. C 2	1861	1864	3
9	80	83	Jose Baca	Sergt	E	1 N. M. Cy	Mch 5, 1864	Oct 15, 1866	2 6 x
10	91	93	Jose Baldes (Pedro S. de Baldes widow of)	Private	C	39 N. York Infy	May 17, 1861	Apr 14, 1864	2 11 x
11	105	106	Porfirio Amayo (Casilda Medina widow of)	Sergt	A	1 N. Mex. Cav	Oct 31, 1861	May 31, 1863	2 7
12	109	111	Victor Gutierrez	Private	H	1 N. Mex. Vol.	1863	1866	3 x x

No.	Post-Office Address. 10	Disability Incurred. 11	Remarks. 12
1	East Las Vegas San Miguel Co	wounded 3 times, twice at Vicksburg	once at Pemberton once at Bull Run
2	East Las Vegas San Miguel Co	x	His name (color) does not exist in Michigan
3	West Las Vegas San Miguel Co	not examined	This man enlisted as a Theodore
4	West Las Vegas San Miguel Co	Shot himself through the hand	Knows not well the month or year
5	West Las Vegas San Miguel Co	was wounded near Ft. Wingate 1863	No Pension and yet has made application
6	West Las Vegas San Miguel Co	don't recall well Enlisted or discharged	This man served in Capt Lavery 1 N.M. Vol
7	West Las Vegas S. Miguel Co	Capt. Simpson of Taos	Lost his discharge
8	West Las Vegas San Miguel County	This man don't recollect dates of his enlistment nor discharge	Lost discharge
9	West Las Vegas " "		Lost his discharge by Flood, date 18th May, 189_
10	West Las Vegas San Miguel County	This man is very poor and needy	had one of his legs amputated
11	West Las Vegas San Miguel County	Porfirio Amayo was sick being dead	This woman poor & needy
12	West Las Vegas San Miguel County	3/4 blind	Receiving Pension but are to have increase

Source: *Eleventh Census of the U.S. Jose Baca #9. Special Schedule San Miguel County New Mexico Territory.*

John Harrison:

Figure: Harrison Country store in Pecos, N.M. About 1884.

Figure: Adelo Country Store which may have been the Harrison Country Store [John Harrison] around 1884. Source: "Pecos mi Pecos", Aspectos Culturales 2002, Roberto Mondragón, Georgia Roybal. Courtesy George Adelo [photo].

Figure: A Left to Right possibly three of the Adelo's, and possibly John Harrison and spouse house in Pecos. Source: "Pecos mi Pecos" 2002, Roberto Mondragon and Georgia Roybal, Aspectos Culturales. Photo by George Adelo.

Dionicio Castillo:

APPLICATION FOR MARRIAGE LICENSE

No. 4656

STATE OF NEW MEXICO, } ss.
County of San Miguel.

TO THE PROBATE CLERK:

I hereby make application for a license to unite in marriage with _Dionicio Castillo_ whose age is _22_ years. I certify I was born at _Chaperito_ on the ___ day of _Agosto_, 1902; that I am now a resident of _Las Vegas N.M._; that we are not related within the degree prohibited by the laws of this State; that neither of us are bound by marriage to another; that there exists no legal impediment to said marriage.

Subscribed and sworn to before me, this _4th_ day of _Nov_ A.D. 1922.

Miquelita Tapia her mark
Perfecto Gallegos Probate Clerk
By _Vidal Flores_ Deputy

[SEAL]

I hereby make application for a license to unite in marriage with _Miquelita Tapia_ whose age is _20_ years. I certify I was born at _Anton Chico_ on the _4_ day of _October_, 1902; that I am now a resident of _Tecolotita_; that we are not related within the degree prohibited by the laws of this State; that neither of us are bound by marriage to another; that there exists no legal impediment to said marriage.

Subscribed and sworn to before me, this _4th_ day of _Nov_ A.D. 1922.

Dionicio Castillo
Perfecto Gallegos Probate Clerk
By _Vidal Flores_ Deputy

Witness to mark
A. D. Garcia
[SEAL]

CONSENT OF PARENT OR GUARDIAN
(Where Either Party is Under Age)

No. _____

I, the parent (or guardian) of _____, hereby consent to the granting of a license to marry, waiving the question of minority.

MARRIAGE LICENSE

No. 4654

STATE OF NEW MEXICO, } ss.
County of San Miguel.

TO ANY PERSON AUTHORIZED BY LAW TO PERFORM THE MARRIAGE CEREMONY, GREETING:
YOU ARE HEREBY AUTHORIZED TO JOIN IN MARRIAGE _Dionicio Castillo_, of _Tecolotita N.M._, and _Miquelita Tapia_, of _Las Vegas_, and of this License you will make due return to my office within the time prescribed by law.

WITNESS my hand and the seal of said Court, at Las Vegas, N. M., this _7_ day of _Nov_, 1922.

Perfecto Gallegos Probate Clerk
By _Vidal Flores_ Deputy

[SEAL]

Recorded _April 17_, 1923, at _11_ A.M., in Marriage Record Book No. _10_ Page No. _4654_
P. Gallegos Probate Clerk and Ex-Officio County Recorder.
By _Vidal Flores_ Deputy

MARRIAGE CERTIFICATE

STATE OF NEW MEXICO, } ss.
County of San Miguel.

I hereby certify that on the _6_ day of _Nov_, A.D. 1922, at _E. Las Vegas_ in said County and State, I, the undersigned, a _Catholic Priest_, did join in the HOLY BONDS OF MATRIMONY, in accordance with the Laws of the State of New Mexico, and the authorization of the following License, _Dionicio Castillo_ of _Tecolotita N. Mex_ and _Miquelita Tapia_ of _Las Vegas_.

WITNESS my hand and seal, the day and year last above written.

Alejandro Mirabal Witnesses
Tomasita Mirabal

(Official Title) _Pastor_
(Signed) _Dionicio Castillo_ Groom
(Signed) _Miquelita Tapia_ Bride

Recorded this _17_ day of _April_, A.D. 1923, at _11_ M., in Marriage Record Book No. _10_,
Page No. _4654_
Antonio D. Gallegos Probate Clerk and Ex-Officio County Recorder.
By _Vidal Flores_ Deputy

Source: Marriage License County of San Miguel, State of New Mexico, Dionicio Castillo and Miquelita Tapia.

Miquelita Tapia Family:

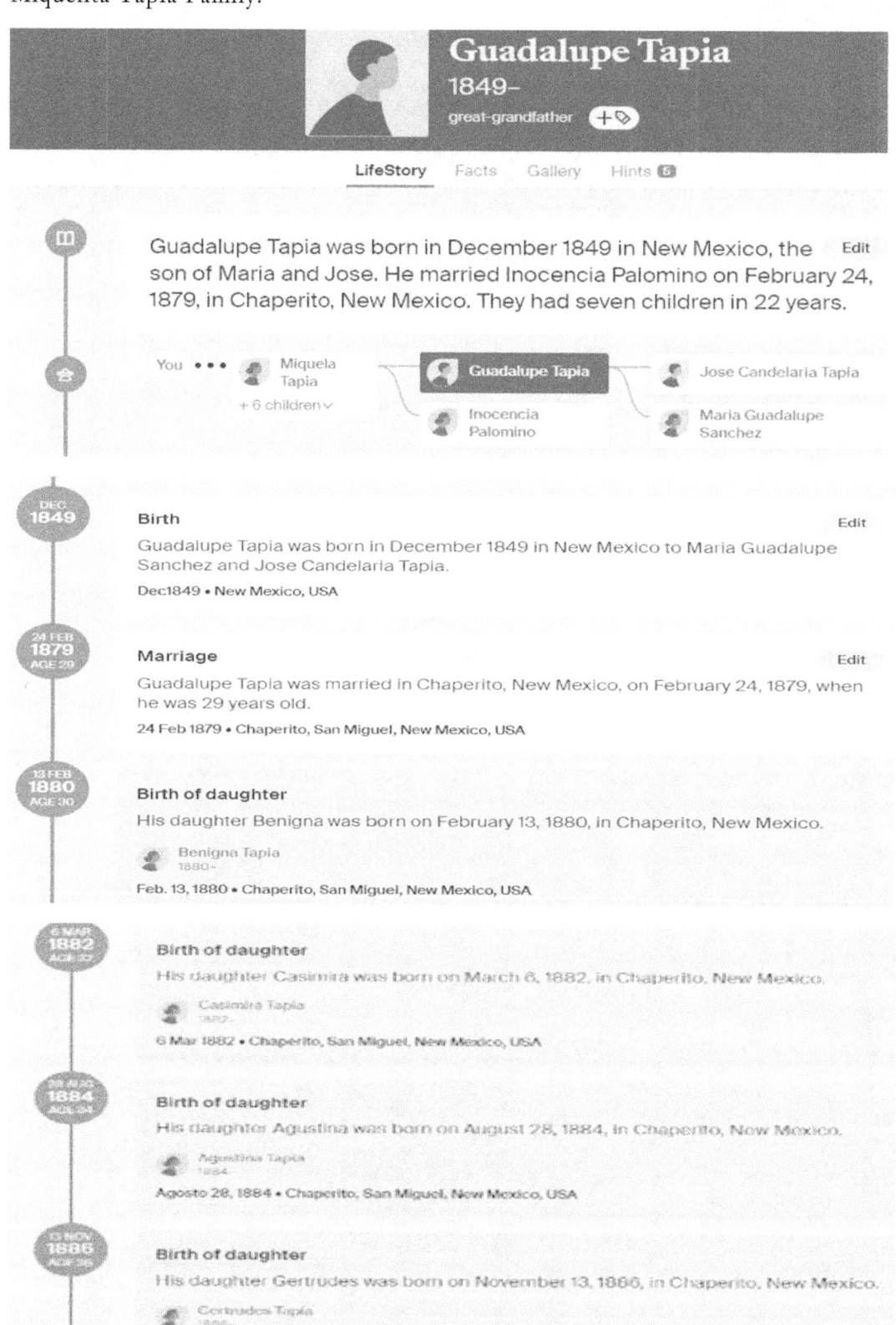

Source: Guadalupe Tapia, Family Tree, Ancestry.

Figure: Maria de los Reyes Lucero Castillo [Mother of Rumaldita Castillo Fresquez]. Courtesy of Theresa Padilla.

Maria de los Reyes Lucero was born in 1885, Anton Chico, N. M. her parents Benigno Lucero and Victoria Baca.

Figure: Rumaldita Castillo Fresquez. Courtesy of Theresa Padilla.   *Figure: Manuelita Carillo Castillo, Dionicio Castillo.*

Rumaldita Castillo Fresquez daughter of Juan de Mata Castillo and Maria de los Reyes Lucero Castillo. Dionicio Castillo is the son of Juan de Mata Castillo and Serafina Romo Castillo.

Figure: Left to right. Manuelita Carillo Castillo, Florian Castillo, Dionicio Castillo. Courtesy Jose M. Castillo.

Florian was in the U.S. Army from 1971-1972.

Basic training was in Fort Ord California. Trained as an ammunition Specialist.

La Banda Flor:

Figure: Left to right. [Standing] Florian, Charlie, [sitting] Mauricio, Tony. [Castillo brothers].

Demetrio Carrillo:

Figure: Demetrio Carillo. Courtesy. José Mauricio Castillo. **Demetrio Carrillo, in the New Mexico, U.S., World War I Records, 1917-1919.**

Don Cruz Lucero:

Figure: Left to right. Cruz Lucero, Rose Ortega Lucero, baby Luis. Front Juan, Maria. Figure: Ramona Martinez Lucero [Mrs. Reymundo Lucero].

Veteran: Yes

Household Members (Name)	Age	Relationship
Cruz Lucero	**67**	**Head (carpenter)**
Rosa Lucero	40	Wife
Juan D Lucero	20	Son
Luis Lucero	14	Son
Reymundo Lucero	12	Son
Cleotilde Lucero	10	Daughter
Merejildo Lucero	6	Son
Ernesto Lucero	4	Son

Source: Ancestry, 1930 U.S. Census, Anton Chico Arriba, Guadalupe County, N.M.

Mrs. Eva Aragon:

Figure: Left to Right. Class of 1966 on a field trip. Mrs. Eva Aragon, Mrs. Rose Sisneros Aguilar. Courtesy Rose Mary Urioste.

Principal:

Mrs. Eva Aragon was the first local Hispanic female Principal in the Anton Chico School.

During those days it was difficult to begin school as a student in pre-primer around 1957. The home language was Spanish. It was required to speak English at school! That was a problem for me because you weren't allowed to ask to be excused to go to the bathroom in Spanish. I didn't know how to ask in English. And wearing pecheras [overalls] didn't help either. Thank goodness my accident was only a number one. Speaking Spanish was simply forbidden.

By the time I was in about first grade my parents were getting ready to go to San Jon to work in the broom fields. Although school was about to begin, and we would be registering a month or so later. My parents got a visit from Mrs. Aragon and Mrs. Marquez as we were getting ready to go to San Jon. Both Mrs. Aragon and Mrs. Marquez were concerned about our education. I believe we got excused for that season until the work in San Jon ended. The work at the broom fields was important to maintain the family's needs for the winter. Although working at the escardas [hoeing cotton in Texas] was the summer migration for my family.

School Lunch:

The school served local fruits and vegetables at the cafeteria provided by the parents and community. Whatever available produce that the parents had access to were encouraged to provide to the school as the lunch payment. Apples, plums, and chile were provided by Juan Tenorio. Mr. Mike Gonzales also took boxes of apples from his orchard. Edwardo, Boni and Ernesto Lucero provided chile. Canning some fruit was a part of the school program. Prior to beginning of school.

Chile stew was in the menu sometimes with meat or with potatoes. The food was good and nutritious.

During the school year a birthday cake was baked monthly at the school cafeteria. The cake was huge, about 18x36 inches. Every month a special table was filled with all the children that celebrated their birthday that month. And the birthday song was sung in celebration. Mrs. Rita Maestas Marquez and Mrs. Escolastica Gutierrez Ulibarri played the piano for special occasions.

A daily prayer was said in unison before lunch at school:

Thank you for the food we eat.

Thank you for the world so sweet.

Thank you for the birds that sing.

Thank you, God for everything.

Figure: Left to Right: Becky Jaramillo, Rose Sisneros Aguilar [Teacher]. Courtesy Rosemary Urioste.

Afternoon Recess:

The students had the opportunity to buy a glass of milk or chocolate milk for two cents. A small bag of potato chips could be purchased for a nickel. The snack was great for the afternoon recess!

When getting on the bus. My aunt Ambrosia shouted in the bus, "tienes que darme dos centavos para la chocolate" to one of her brothers.

Discipline:

Jr. got in trouble often. Sometimes his father came into the principal's office and the principal disciplined him in front of his father.

On another occasion he got sent to the office, which was a good thing. Cousin Frances was secretary, and in charge she simply gave him permission to get a bag of potato chips to snack on. Jr. got a bag of chips and crushed them between book pages pages to conceal the snack. Frances also offered him some new pencils.

Miguel Gonzales:

Figure: Left to Right. Louie, Otilia, Michael, and Miguel Gonzales. Courtesy Rosemary Urioste

Miguel Gonzales was the eighth-grade teacher in Anton Chico. For many years he coached basketball on an outside court. During out-of-town games he took the team on the back of his Chevy truck with a camper shell.

Figure: Faustin Aguilar [father of Otilia Gonzales. Courtesy Rosemary Urioste.

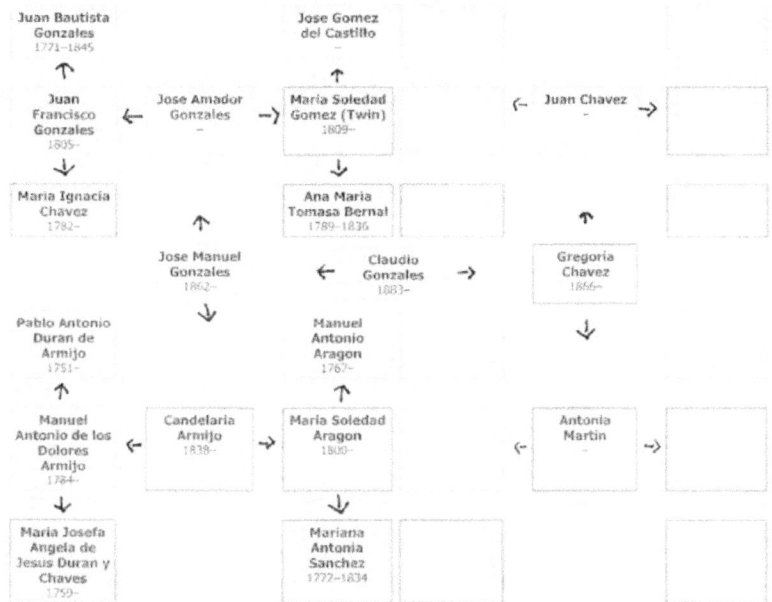

Source: HGRC Compact Tree [Claudio Gonzales].

Don Tomas Maestas:

Figure: Tomas Maestas. Courtesy Tomasito Maestas.   Figure: Guadalupe Gonzales Maestas. Courtesy Tomasito Maestas.

Household Members	Age	Relationship
Tomas Maestas	37	Head
Guadalupe Maestas	34	Wife
Juliana Maestas	14	Daughter
Estela Maestas	12	Daughter
Juan Maestas	10	Son
Jesus M Maestas	**8**	**Son**
Nazario Maestas	6	Son
Rita Maestas	3	Daughter
Cristian Maestas	1	Son
Ventura Maestas	90	Grandfather

1920 U.S Census Family Home: Cuervo, Guadalupe, N.M.

Source: Ancestry / 1920 U.S. Census Cuervo Guadalupe County New Mexico.

Household Members	Age	Relationship
Tomas Maestas	48	Head
Guadalupe G Maestas	43	Wife
Juan Maestas	20	Son
Jesus Maestas	18	Son
Nazario Maestas	16	Son
Rita Maestas	14	Daughter
Cristian Maestas	**12**	**Son**
Carlos Maestas	9	Son
Eloisa/Eliza Maestas	7	Daughter
Roberto Maestas	3	Son

1930 U.S. Census Family Home: Anton Chico Arriba, Guadalupe, N.M.

Source: Ancestry / 1930 U.S. Census Cuervo Guadalupe County New Mexico.

Figure: 1936 Wedding Padrino Jesus Maestas, Groom Juan Maestas, Estelita, Madrina Rita Maestas Marquez, Bella Maestas Pino, Grabielita Pino, Emma Gutierrez Contreras, Emma Marquez, Bennie Gutierrez Rios, Herlinda Gutierrez Sisneros, Maria. Courtesy Anthony Maestas.

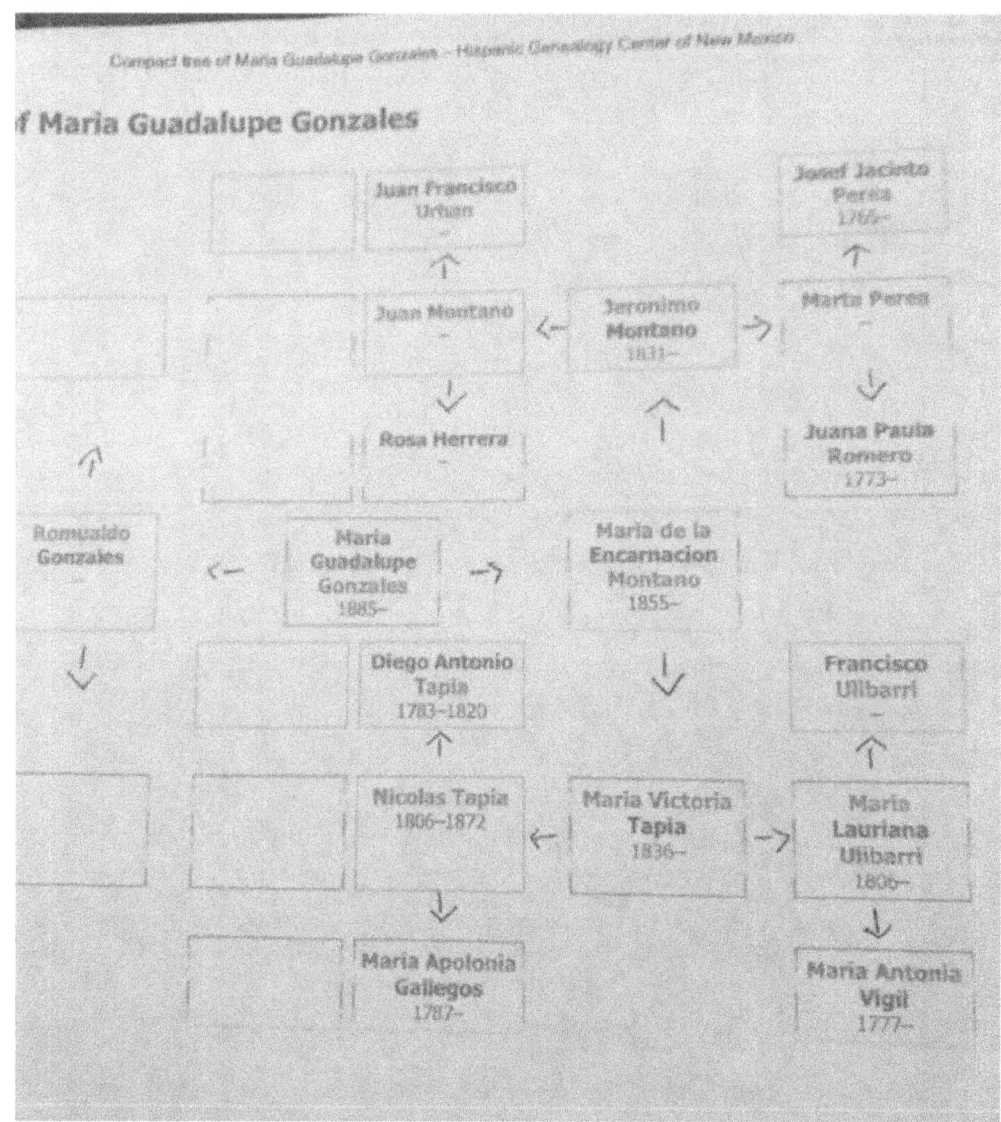

Source: www.hgrc-nm.org/webtrees/compact.

Household Members	Age	Relationship
Rumaldo Gonzales	51	Head
Chonita Gonzales	45	Wife
Pedro Gonzales	16	Son
Guadalupe Gonzales	**14**	**Daughter**
Benigno Gonzales	11	Son
Clarita Gonzales	6	Daughter
Enriquez Salazar	2	Nephew

1900 U.S. Census Family Home: Pajarito, Guadalupe, N.M.
   Source: Ancestry / 1900 U.S. Census Cuervo Guadalupe County New Mexico.

Household Members	Age	Relationship
MA Guadalupe Gonzales	60	
MA Miquela Gonzales	40	
Rumaldo Gonzales	**12**	
Jose Lino Gonzales	10	
Tomasa Gonzales	6	

1860 U.S. Census Family Home: Bernal, San Miguel, N.M. Territory.

Source: Ancestry / 1860 U.S. Census Cuervo Guadalupe County New Mexico.

Figure: Left to right. Jesus Maestas, Juan Maestas, Estelita, Rita Maestas Marquez. Courtesy Anthony Maestas.

Figure: Left to right. Nazario, Juan, Clara, Jesus, Tommy, Natasha. Courtesy Anthony Maestas.

Don Julián Maestas:

Figure: Julian Maestas. Courtesy Nick Maestas.

Figure: Ramoncita Ulibarri Maestas. Courtesy Nick Maestas

Figure: Left to right. Placido Martínez 1872-1964 and Piedad Masetas Martínez [hermana de don Julián Maestas]. Courtesy Rachel Maes.

Figure: Beatriz Maestas Ulibarri [Mamaita] [born April 19, 1885] daughter of Ascencion Lucero and Jesus Maria Maestas. Courtesy Agenda Aragon Pino.

Figure: Left to Right Julian Maestas, Ramoncita Ulibarri Maestas. Courtesy Nick Maestas.

Figure: Left to Right. Jose Leon [Nick's uncle] Margarito Sisneros. Courtesy Nick Maestas.

Name:	Pablita Lucero Sisneros
Age in 1910:	50
Birth Date:	1860[1860]
Birthplace:	New Mexico
Home in 1910:	Anton Chico, Guadalupe, New Mexico, USA
Race:	White
Gender:	Female
Relation to Head of House:	Wife
Marital Status:	Married
Spouse's Name:	Jose Leon Sisneros
Father's Birthplace:	New Mexico
Mother's Birthplace:	New Mexico
Native Tongue:	Spanish
Able to read:	Yes
Able to Write:	No
Years Married:	24

Number of Children Born: 10

Number of Children Living: 8

Household Members	Age	Relationship
Jose Leon Sisneros	54	Head
Pablita Sisneros	**50**	**Wife**
Pracedes Sisneros	24	Son
Margarito Sisneros	22	Son
Rosita Sisneros	20	Daughter
Maria Guadalupe Sisneros	17	Daughter
Andres Sisneros	15	Son
Maria Socorro Sisneros	10	Daughter

Source: Ancestry 1910 U.S. Federal Census Record.

Figure: Left to Right. Back Row. Reymundo Maestas, Prospero Pino, Frank Maestas, Uvaldo Sisneros, Margarito Sisneros, Front Row. Ramoncita Ulibarri Maestas, Bella Maestas Pino, Agneda Sisneros Maestas, Rosa Sisneros Aguilar, Otilia Sisneros, Courtesy Nick Maestas.

Figure: Frank Maestas. Courtesy Nick Maestas.   *Figure: Agneda Sisneros Maestas. Courtesy Nick Maestas.*

Figure: Left to Right. Frank Maestas, Pete Pino, Antonio Maestas. Courtesy Nick Maestas.

Piedad:

Figure: Left to right. Placido Martínez 1872-1964 and Piedad Maestas Martínez [hermana de don Julián Masetas]. Courtesy Rachel Maes.

Captive:

Piedad had been a captive of the Indians. Piedad was a hard worker making her own adobe home. [Rachael Márquez Maes, personal communication, December 24, 2020].

Piedad, Raquel and Papá Tomas:

Piedad cared for Rachel Márquez Maes when Rachel was a little girl. That's what abuelitas did. Piedad la hija de mamá Chonita y papá Tomas. Y hermana de Beatriz M. Ulibarri. Papá Tomas also spent his days with Raquel and Piedad. Tomas was blind by now and liked sitting by the fogón [Wood stove]. Papá Tomas often called Raquel, "Ven paca". But this time he burnt himself on the fogón.

Mamá Piedad lit a candle every night. She also put a mantle on her head during her ritual. One night her dress caught on fire. Tía Clara caught her and helped when she got on fire with the candle.

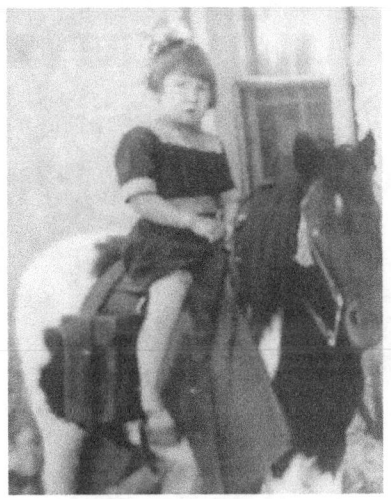

Figure: Rachel Márquez Maes. Courtesy Rachel Márquez Maes.

Dresses made of Flour Sacks:

Raquel's dresses were homemade. The fabric available was usually from the flour sacks Diamond M, Gold Medal, and one other common brand. The prints were usually attractive with flowers and pretty colors. The flour was used and then the sack was ready for cutting and sewing. Tía Mariana Saiz Tafoya prepared Raquel for the school year by sewing all of Raquel's clothes. [Rachael Márquez Maes, personal communication, December 24, 2020].

Don Onofre Marquez:

Figure: Left to right. Unidentified, Marianita Griego Marquez [mother of George Marquez], unidentified, Onofre Marquez holding George Marquez [father of Rachel Marquez Maes]. Courtesy of Rachel Marquez Maes.

MY GREAT-GRANDFATHER Silvestre Marquez on my mother's side during the late 1800s and early 1900s owned a saloon in Anton Chico. his saloon, or cantina, was located just behind St. Joseph's Church in nton Chico.

The back bar seems well stocked. The large hanging kerosene lamp urnished light at nights. You will also note a couple of spitoons at the oot of the bar. It does not show a foot railing as seen in many Western aloons.

You will also note the gentleman with his rifle and powderhorn. He ust not have had to check it at the bar, and was even allowed to

The picture was taken sometime in 1898 or 1e99 and shows, f to right, the following: Eliseo Armijo; El Viejo Johnson, wi Sotero Marquez; son of Silvestre Marquez; Martha Marqu youngest of the Silvestre Marquez family; Don Quiros, standing bar; Silvestre Marquez, the owner; David Marques, anothe Genoveva Marquez, David's daughter, the mother of Soledad of Santa Rosa; Castulo Marquez, another son; and Luis Agu brother of my grandfather, Andres Aguilar, who was married to S Marquez, another of the daughters of Silvestre

The bar was located alongside the old Military Road (used Cavalry and freight wagons between Fort Union, Las Vegas,

Figure: Albuq. Morning Journal Newspaper, Dec. 24, 1904. Clipping. Courtesy of Dennis Marquez.

Figure: Newspaper Clipping. Courtesy Dennis Marquez.

Figure: George Marquez [8th grade graduation], Deluvina Martinez. Courtesy Rachel Maes.

Figure: Deluvina Martinez bride, George Marquez groom, Wedding in Anton Chico 4-28-1919. Courtesy Rachel Marquez Maes

George was a schoolteacher and worked at the Post Office for 40 years.

Figure: Elvira Deluvina Márquez Hafner. Courtesy Rachel Márquez Maes.

Elvira married a Navy Captain.

Figure: Rachel Márquez Maes, Carlos Maes. Courtesy Rachel Márquez Maes.

Figure: Carlos Maes, Shelly Winters [movie star]. Courtesy Rachel Marquez Maes.

Figure: Lee Isaac Márquez. Courtesy Rachel Márquez Maes.

Lee Isaac Márquez a soldier and plane flagstops.

Figure: Lee George Maes [Rachel Maes's son]. Courtesy of Rachel Marquez Maes.

Don Silvestre Marquez:

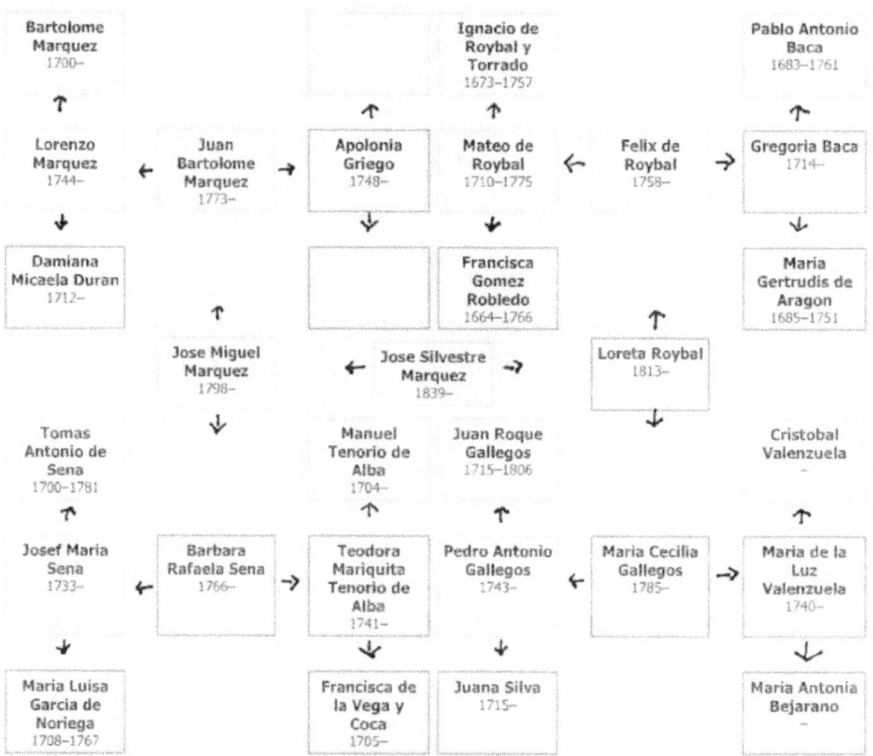

Source: HGRC Compact Tree of Jose Silvestre Marquez.

Figure: Left to Right Silvestre Marquez 11/22/1839 and Teresita Silva Marquez 11/12/1848. Courtesy Dennis Marquez

Doña Manuelita Mink Nelson:

Figure: Manuelita Mink Nelson. Courtesy Mary Sanchez Baca.

Figure: Left to right. Celina Nelson [Mother of Mary Sanchez Baca], Quetita Nelson [teacher], Carolina Nelson [teacher], Charles Nelson, Tony Nelson, Emory Nelson. Courtesy Mary Sanchez Baca.

Figure: Julia Nelson Tenorio [born 1900]. First female Guadalupe County Superintendent. Courtesy Mary Sanchez Baca.

Don Nicasio Sanchez:

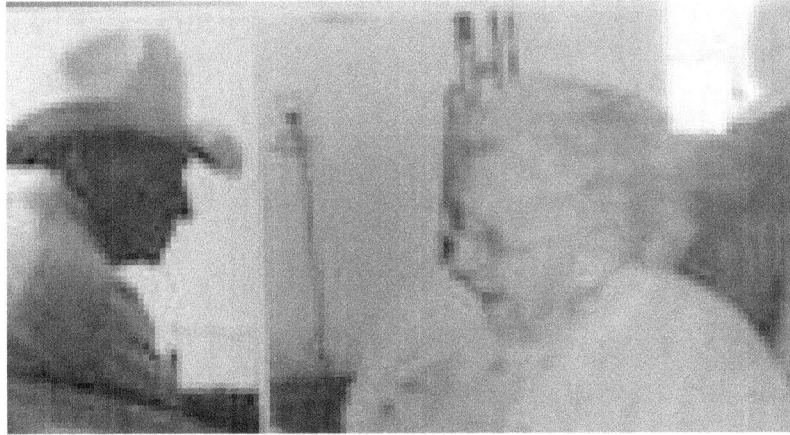

Figure: Left to right. Nicasio Sanchez. Courtesy Nick Maestas.

Taking out hay is hard work, but Nicasio had his help before the season started. Guggie [Ufrendo Jaramillo] often asked Nicasio for money and Nicasio readily loaned out money to his young helpers. Guggie and his friends were anxious and excited for hay season to begin because they knew that they had a job and were ready to repay Nicasio for his generosity on the money loan.

Figure: Sanchez Ranch in Dahlia. Courtesy of Mary Sanchez Baca.

Rodeo Clown:

Weekends and the way of life were the rodeo events at la Luvina the Sanchez Ranch or Manuel Maes Ranch. Horse races were very important also.

Nicasio Sanchez was the rodeo clown. His most important attraction was the springy coil glasses with bulgy eyes. Next, he saddled his caballito bayo, putting the saddle on backwards. Then he pulled the back cinch tight, and the horse took off bucking wildly! When the horse finally stopped Nicasio ran for his horse and climbed on his horse pointing while sitting backwards but this time the horse was walking tame as can be. [Arturo Lucero, personal communication].

Bernardino Baca participated in the rodeo events. Arturo Romero also got lipstick and makeup supplies from his mother and was a clown's makeup artist at la Luvina.

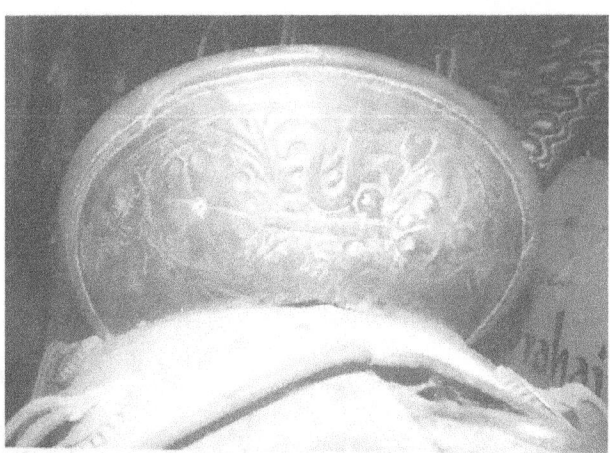

Figure: Julian Sanchez's saddle [great uncle of Mary Sanchez Baca].

The saddle of Julian Sanchez is now owned by Braheim Hindi in Duran, N. M. at El Rancho del Gallo.

Julian died in 1918 of the Spanish flu and buried at El Marino. El Marino is a place named after a cattle rustler from Fort Sumner. [Mary Sanchez Baca, personal communication]

Figure: David J. Baca at El Cerrito bridge after washing out around 1990. Courtesy Mary Sanchez Baca.

Kiko Gutierrez:

Figure: Frank Gutierrez [Kiko]. Courtesy Connie Frances Gutierrez Griego. Figure: Maria Virginia Gallegos 1925-1967. Courtesy Connie Frances Gutierrez Griego.

Figure: Frank Gutierrez on sax. Frank Gutierrez Band. Courtesy Connie Frances Gutierrez Griego.

Heraldo Mondragón and Alfonso Aragón:

Figure: Left to Right Heraldo Mondragon, Alfonso Aragon. Courtesy Tina Lucero Aragon.

La Toyota:

Heraldo and Alfonso were close friends they hunted and went for leña [wood] together. Heraldo had his yellow 1960's short-bed Toyota pick-up truck. On his Toyota he got wood for the winter. Heraldo was fond of his Toyota. Even though it was just a pick-up he would often say, "es como una zorra donde quiera se trepa".

El Chainsaw:

Heraldo used wood for cooking in his woodstove all year long, but Heraldo's chainsaw gave him troublesome times. And while working on the saw at the Community Center he explained to the men "it starts and stays on idle". The men wanted to know if the saw was cutting and if it got speed when giving it gas. Then Heraldo said, "sí está se desmorese". But when I put it on the log it loses power.

Hunting:

Hunting at the monte was also a part of life. Both Alfonso and Heraldo went on hunting trips. Tina often prepared a pile of blankets. And Heraldo often laughed at the pile of blankets and counted. His count was about ten blankets. [Tina Lucero Aragon, personal communication, August 2018].

Volkswagen:

On a trip to La mesa del Medio Heraldo was on his Volkswagen. The cuesta is steep and Heraldo had some big men with him, "unos gordos". Nick Hern and the others wanted to get out of the Volkswagen. Heraldo knew the car would make it up the mesa. And the car went up con tuy gordos. [Father Mondragon, personal communication, July 2018].

Figure: Left to Right Alfonso Aragon, Joe Aragon / Korea. Courtesy Tina Lucero Aragon.

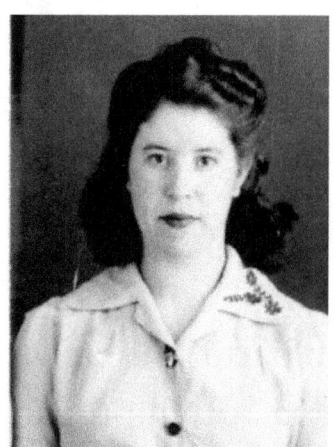 

Figure: Left to Right Frances Aragon Garcia, Irene Aragon. Courtesy Tina Lucero Aragón.

Don Juan Bautista Olguin:

Figure: Left to right standing. Perfecto Olguin, Cecilio Olguin [brothers], Benigno Castillo [brother-in-law]. Middle Row standing] Victoriana Baca, [sitting] Juan Bautista Olguin, Victoria Lucero [parents]. Victoriana Baca, Marcelina Castillo, Apolonia Olguin [baby]. Courtesy Sara López.

Figure: Silverina Olguin Romo. Courtesy Sara López.

Source: *Family Tree. Courtesy Maggie Romo Cordova.*

Figure: *Patricio Olguin, Josefa Romo. Married San Miguel, N.M. 2-19-1917. Courtesy Betty Olguin.*

Figure: Ramona Olguin 17yrs [dau. of Pat. Olguin & Josefa Romo], from Dahlia. Procopio Montoya 22 yrs. [son of Felipe Montoya & Reyes Lucero from Tecolotito]. Married 12-27-1939. Courtesy Betty Olguin.

Figure: Eutemio Garcia, clipping. Courtesy Rosemary Urioste.

Don Timoteo Leyba:

Figure: Left to Right. Grandpa Timoteo Leyba, Bobby. Bernice, Ernie, [kids of Benny Leyba].

Figure: Grandma Rumaldita Leyba [a midwife]. Courtesy of Maria Otero.

Figure: Grabielita Leyba Otero, [daughter of T. Leyba & Rumalda Bustamante]. Serafín Otero, [son of Serafín Otero & María Encinias] Marriage on Jan. 31, 1921 Antón Chico Yglesia de San José. Courtesy of María Otero.

Figure: Left to Right: Serafín Otero, Grabielita Leyba Otero, baby Eulogio [first child]. Courtesy of Maria Otero.

Teacher en Tecolotito:

Grabielita, attended la Normal [NMHU] and later taught third grade in Tecolotito. Don Boni Baca was one of her students during her career.

Serafin was a sheepherder. [Maria Otero, personal communication, July 17, 2019].

The Captive:

Isidro Otero had been taken captive by Natives. Isidro Otero was born in 1832. For twelve years he was gone. The family was after the Natives in search of Isidro. When they finally got Isidro back his hair was long, blond, and braided. Isidro said to the family, "manofuchile aqui ay mucho zaragate[grass]". The family had related the story to Maria. [Maria Otero, personal communication, July 17, 2019].

Name	Sex	Age	Birth Year (Estimated)	Birthplace	Marital Status	Occupation	Race	Relationship to Head of Household	Father's
Trinidad Greallgo	Male	34	1846	New Mexico, United States	Married	Farmer	White	Self	New Mex States
Inana O Greallgo	Female	28	1852	New Mexico, United States	Married		White	Wife	New Mex States
Levera Greallgo	Female	12	1868	New Mexico, United States	Single		White	Daughter	New Mex States
Francisco Greallgo	Male	5	1875	New Mexico, United States	Single		White	Son	New Mex States
Leandra Greallgo	Female	4	1876	New Mexico, United States	Single		White	Daughter	New Mex States
Antonio Greallgo	Male	0	1880	New Mexico, United States	Single		White	Son	New Mex States
Isidro Otero	Male	48	1832	New Mexico, United States		Sheep Raiser	White	Self	New Mex States
Donaciana Otero	Female	19	1861	New Mexico, United States			White	Daughter	New Mex States
Serafin Otero	Male	16	1864	New Mexico, United States			White	Son	New Mex States
Apollonio Otero	Male	14	1866	New Mexico, United States			White	Son	New Mex States

Source: United States, Family Search 1880 Census Las Vegas, New Mexico.

Figure: Left to Right. Grabielita Leyba Otero and [brother] Benerito Leyba. Courtesy of Maria Otero.

Figure: Left to right. Bersabe Romero Villanueva, and Mother Rosa Baca Romero, Grabielita Leyba Otero, Rodolfo Otero behind car. Courtesy of Maria Otero.

Figure: Left to Right. María Otero, Isidro, Ercilia Otero, Rodolfo Otero [siblings of María Otero]. Courtesy of Maria Otero.

Figure: Left to Right. Betty, Rudy [Rodolfo Otero and Lisbe Cordova Otero's kids]

Figure: María Otero. Courtesy María Otero.   *Figure: María Otero. Courtesy María Otero.*

Maria Otero lived in Tecolotito and sometimes walked to Anton Chico to buy food that was needed by the family.

Figure: Left to Right. Tillie, Isidro Otero Sr. Aug. 7, 1933-Apr. 5, 2007. Courtesy of María Otero.

Figure: Left to Right. John Pat Otero [son] of Maria Otero. Courtesy of Maria Otero.

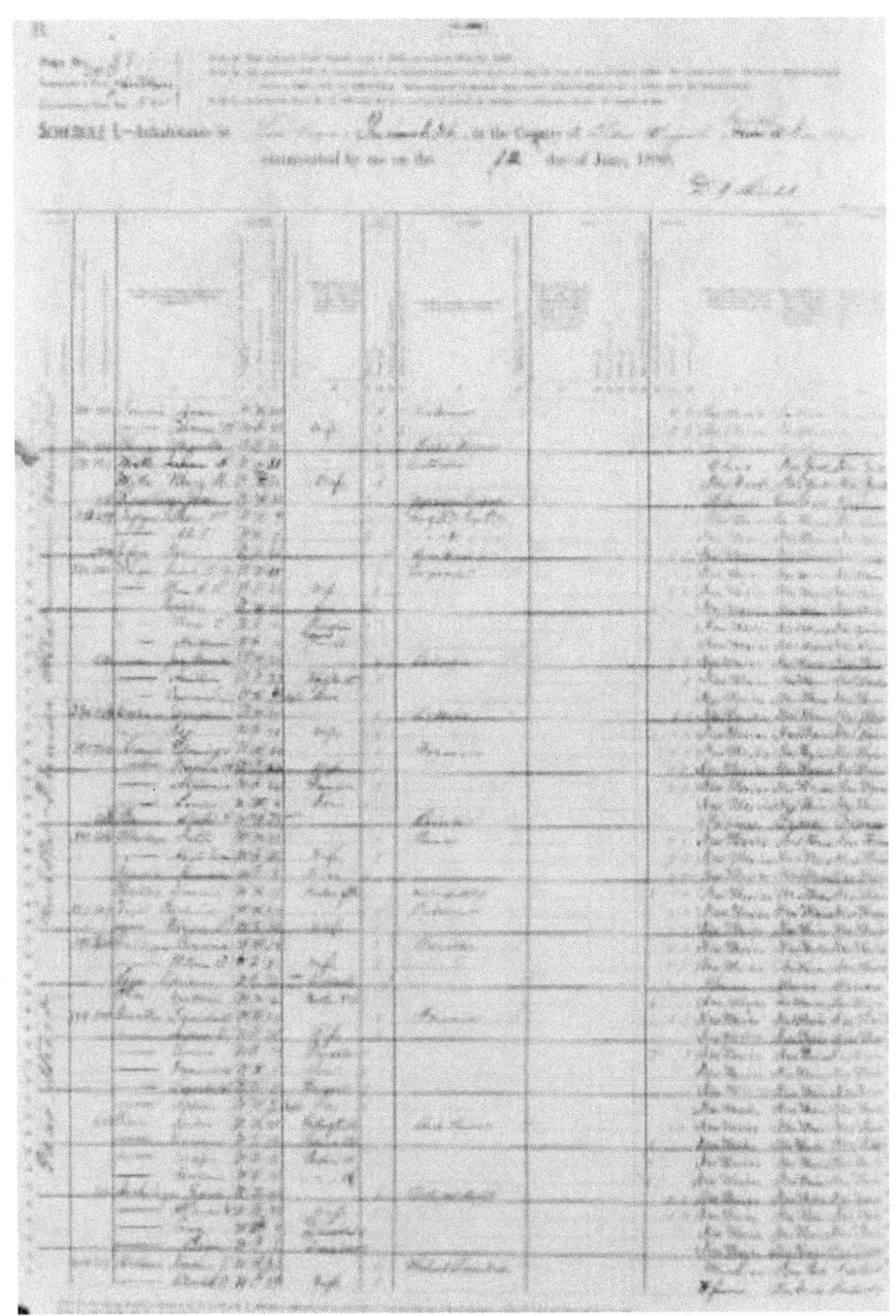

Source: United States, Family Search 1880 Census Las Vegas, New Mexico.

Figure: Jacqueline Otero Henderson [granddaughter] of Josie Otero. Figure: Patricia Ann Pacheco-Gurule. 3/ 5/, 1979 – 1/ 3/ 2009. Courtesy Maria Otero.

Don Samuel Pino:

Source: Newspaper clipping Courtesy Natasha J. Lopez.

Source: Newspaper clipping Courtesy Natasha J. Lopez.

 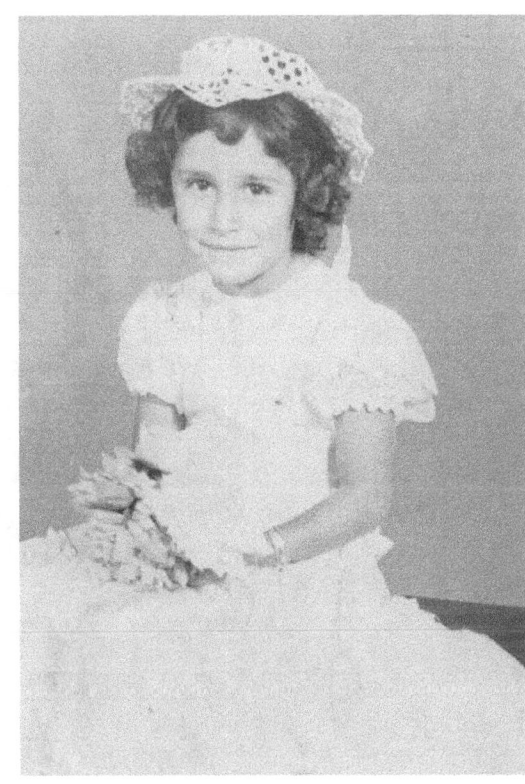

Figure: Julia Montaño Maestas. Courtesy Natasha J. Lopez.   *Figure: Julia Montaño Maestas. Courtesy Natasha J. Lopez.*

Source: Newspaper clipping. Courtesy Agneda Aragon Pino.

Figure: Abelino Pino. Holding a .44 Winchester and the note was found in the stock. Courtesy of Agneda Araaon Pino.

Source: Newspaper clippings. Courtesy Agneda Aragon Pino.

Don Esteban Romero:

Figure: Esteban Romero. World War II. Courtesy Alice Villanueva Chavez.

War:

Esteban Romero was preparing for war. His mother Doña Apolonita was a devout and religious person with many beliefs. Apolonita believed that with a medal of San Antonio, Esteban would be safe upon his return from Germany. Apolonita also believed that perhaps putting the statue of Saint Anthony in a suitcase for Esteban's safe return home from war. But the promise of the return of Esteban would include taking the statue out of enclosure when he returned home.

Esteban was now in Germany and lost his medal of Saint Anthony that Apolonita had given him to wear.

The hardships were many during the time of service. His helmet was now used for drinking water from the available water holes.

Apolonita prayed for the return of Esteban. One day a mysterious movement within the suitcase occurred. No explanation at all and perhaps it was a sign.

And without anyone knowing Esteban arrived home. He had also managed to bring his helmet. Esteban's only daughter Bersabe always kept and treasured the WWII helmet that her father had worn.

His stomach was not well. And his hair loss was another problem that he would now deal with. But he was now home. [Mary Alice Villanueva Chavez, personal communication, Nov. 17, 2019].

Figure: Headstone of Estevan Romero. Courtesy Alice Villanueva Chavez.

Figure: Bersabe Romero Villanueva. Courtesy Alice Villanueva Chavez.

Figure: Left to right. Bersabe Romero Villanueva, Cipriano Villanueva. Tecolotito Dec. 1960. Courtesy Alice Villanueva Chavez.
Figure: Cipriano Villanueva. 1961. Courtesy Alice Villanueva Chavez

Figure: *Anastacia Romero, José Filimon Romero.* Figure: *Santiago Romero, Josefina Romero, Johnny Encinias. Courtesy Arturo Romero.*

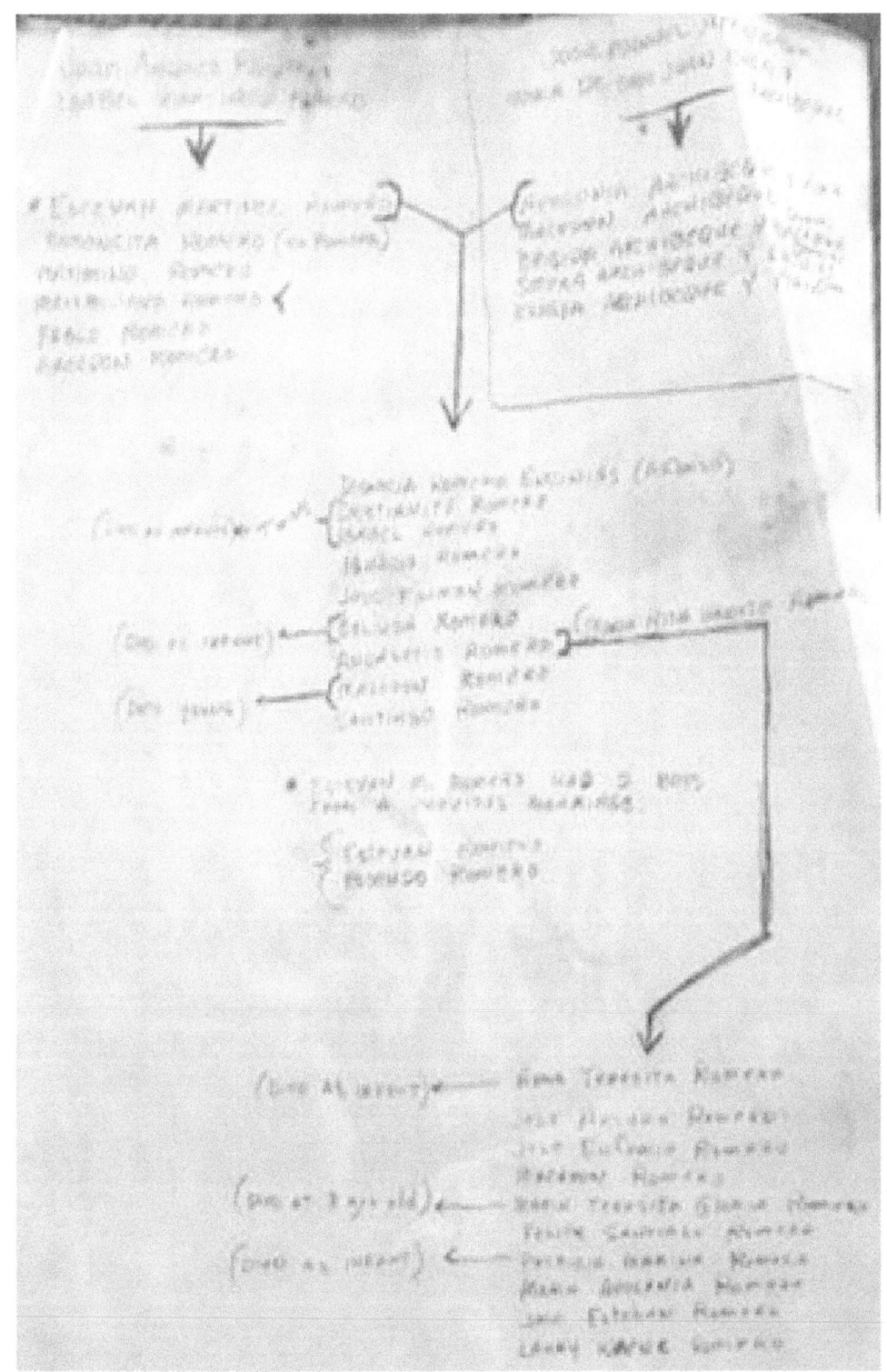

Source: Romero Family Tree. Courtesy Beverly Lucero Baca.

Source: Ancestry U.S. Census 1870.

Figure: Left to Right. Cipriano Villanueva, Alfonso Encinias. Figure: Cipriano Villanueva, Bersabe Romero Villanueva. Tecolotito Dec. 1960. Courtesy Alice Villanueva Chavez.

Figure: Tomacita Abeyta Baca, Benjamin Baca [brother of Rosa Baca, uncle of Bersabe Romero Villanueva] Courtesy Alice Villanueva Chavez.

Wyoming:

Figure: Cipriano Villanueva. In Wyoming @ Mr. Boller Apr. 1967. Courtesy Mary Alice Villanueva Chavez.

En La Borrega:

    Don Cipriano and David travelled to Wyoming from Tecolotito spending several months there. The work was all about the borrega. Herding sheep in the llanos and sometimes even building a mojonera [rock piles] to keep a sense of direction during bad weather and fog.

    Tenía que híjar [birthing] las borregas. Andaba de tasinque y trasquilador [clip wool] de borregas. La borrega la protegían del frio con la manta [a canvas cover]. The work was hard during those cold months.

Figure: Left to Right. Carlos Villanueva, unidentified, David Villanueva. Picture at Yellowstone Park. Courtesy Mary Alice Villanueva Chavez.

Figure: Left to right. Back row Cipriano Villanueva, Manuel Villanueva, Bersabe Romero Villanueva, Rebecca Chavez Villanueva, Joe 2yrs. 5 mos. Pic. Taken 1945. Courtesy Alice Villanueva Chavez.

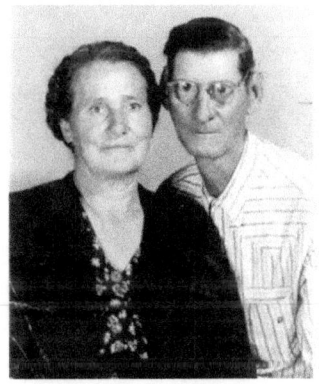

Figure: Left to Right. Rebecca Chavez Villanueva, Manuel Villanueva. Courtesy Alice Villanueva Chavez.

Figure: Marcelina Montoya [mother of Rebecca Chavez Villanueva]. Courtesy Alice Villanueva Chavez.

Female
Birth • •
28 April 1870
New Mexico, United States
Christening • •
28 April 1870
Nuestra Senora De Los Angeles-Catholic, Pecos, San Miguel, New Mexico
Death • •
1917
San Juan, San Miguel, New Mexico, United States

Figure: Left to right. Pedro Gallegos, Claudine Gallegos, Vivianna Chavez, Tranquilino Chavez, Rebecca Chavez Villanueva and Pablo Chavez. Courtesy Alice Villanueva Chavez

Figure: Left to right. Corrina Carrillo Tenorio, Bersabe Romero Villanueva. [Recipes for home canning 7/12/2011]. Courtesy Alice Villanueva Chavez.

Figure: Left to right. Louisa Baca Lucero, Bersabe Romero Villanueva, Lila Baca Lucero. Courtesy Mary Alice Villanueva Chavez.

Figure: Back Left to Right. Joe Villanueva, Felipe Tenorio, Maximiliano Tenorio. Front Left to Right. Cipriano Villanueva Jr. Rosa Villanueva, Gabby Villanueva Velásquez, [Baby] Chavela Encinias. Courtesy Alice Villanueva Chavez.

Figure: Henry Villanueva. [Army].

Figure: Manuel Villanueva, [Army April 1976]. Courtesy Mary Alice Villanueva Chavez

11/21/1963 Ft. Ord. Calif.

Pabla Medina:

Pabla is the daughter of J. Medina and Juana Baca. [St. Joseph's Catholic Church Anton Chico, N. Mex.]

A visit with Pabla was a treat because walking into her casita next door gave you a feeling of awe and admiration. Pabla had a goat skin rug in front of her black and white television. Alice sat on the rug and watched television. Pabla had a warm and welcoming casita. Sometimes serving Alice a cup of tea.

And in front of her casita, she had a black Model A. Pabla's Model A ran well and at times she drove people to the doctor. [Mary Alice Villanueva Chavez, personal communication, Nov. 17, 2019].

Doña Tiburcia Jaramillo Olguin Castillo:

Tiburcia Jaramillo [baptized April 22, 1866] the daughter of Juan Jose de Jesus Jaramillo born in 1825 and Juana Antonia Urioste born in 1833. Pascual Jaramillo was her brother he was born around 1861. [St. Joseph's Catholic Church Anton Chico, N. Mex.]

Selling Atole:

Rick Romo's grandma Tiburcia Jaramillo was born at Viandante. Tiburcia married Jesus Olguin on Dec. 7, 1884. [St. Joseph's Catholic Church Anton Chico, N. Mex.] Census records show Tiburcia lived in Viandante till 1899.

The Viandante was a busy place. Soldiers had a rock corral at the crossing, and they traveled to Fort Union.

Tiburcia made a little money by selling atole [blue cornmeal] to the soldiers. A cup of atole for 3 or 5 cents. She poured the atole into their canteens. [Rick Romo, personal communication, June 16, 2019].

Tiburcia was widowed and married Concepcion Castillo from Tecolotito in 1899.

River Crossing at Cerrito de la Cueva:

Harina de maiz was an important food source for everyone. Doña Emilia Romero Baca [born in 1908] and Apolonita Archibeque Romero molian maiz para harina.

The two women worked hard. Emilia and Apolonita crossed carretas with the mules at la Cueva del Padre. [Arturo Romero, personal communication, July 7, 2018].

> Page 259. Abril 19 de 1886.
> Bautize a **María Apolinia Archeveque**, hija legitima de José Archeveque y de María de San Juan Baca, de Tecolotito. Padrinos: Francisco Mártinez y María Eugenia Mora.
>
> Page 9 Line 45. Abril 21 de 1888.
> Bautize a **María Sotera Archeveque**, nacida en Anton Chico en Abril 20 de 1888, hija legitima de José Manuel Archeveque y de María Juana Baca. Padrinos: José Vicente Martín y María Teodora Incinias.
>
> Page 23 Line 63. Junio 19 de 1890.
> Bautize a **Antonia Archeveque**, nacida en Tecolotito, en Junio 7 de 1890, hija legitima de José Archeveque y de María de San Juan Baca. Padrinos: Francisco Gonzáles y María Ale. Urioste.
>
> Page 30 Line 84.

Source: New Mexico Baptisms Anton Chico, La Yglesia de San Jose 1857-1897.

Don Felipe Romo el Caporal:

Un señor andaba buscando trabajo de borregero con Manuel Urias el español. Manuel tenia el trabajo mas en demanda para los hombres. El señor andaba en busca de trabajo con Manuel Urias y le dijo "sí te doy trabajo". "Ve al Palo Amarillo y donde mires a un hombre alto y largo como un papolote". 'Ese es Felipe Romo el Caporal". "Hay es el campo". "Dile que yo te despache". [Reymundo Maestas, personal communication, April 3, 2007]. Felipe Romo abuelo de Rick Romo.

Rick Romo in Thule Greenland:

Figure: Front Rick Romo. Courtesy Lugie Romo.

Figure: Rick Romo. Courtesy Lugie Romo.

Rick at 17 years of age and trained at Fort Carson in Colorado Springs. Then later trained at Fort Bliss Texas.

He was now with the "Army Guided Missiles".

Rick's assignment was to prepare missiles for flight and to protect the missiles. There were four missile sites.

By train he got to the Bay Area in San Francisco, California. Now stationed and where he spent 3 years.

On his last year he was flown to New Jersey and then the military flew Rick past the Arctic Circle to Thule, Greenland. 3,000 miles from Russia. His job was to take care of the missiles.

Rick was now in "The Land of the Midnight Sun". 3 months of no sun, 3 months of day and night, 3 months of night and day then, 3 months of no sun. Rick saw the swirls of green, blue, yellow, or pink shimmer pulsating across the night sky dancing. Best seen in mid-September and peaking in March because of the long dark nights. He observed the colorful Northern Lights and the purple streak of lights when the sun was no longer going to come out. Service to the USA [his country] from 1955 to 1959. [Rick Romo, personal communication, June 16, 2019].

Figure: Feeding White Arctic Fox, Rick Romo. Courtesy Lugie Romo.

Don Alejandro Bachicha:

Figure: Left to right. Front row Agneda, Helen, Mary, Pablita, Piedad, Alejandro, Zenaida, Adela, Phoebe. George Lupe, Willie, and Celestriano. Courtesy Virginia Quintana.

Figure: Left to right front. Zenaida Bachicha Raybon, Piedad Bachicha. Back Sylvia, Bob, Corrine. Courtesy Virginia Quintana.

Figure: Agneda Bachicha Sandoval and Frank Sandoval. Courtesy Rosanna Martinez Madero.

Amigos:

Figure: Mike Stevens Vietnam Veteran. Courtesy Gloria Stevens.

Figure: Mike Stevens. Courtesy Gloria Stevens.

Figure: Gloria and Mike Stevens wedding. Figure: Gloria and Mike Stevens 50th anniversary Dec. 2021. Courtesy Gloria Stevens.

Mike is a Vietnam Veteran and is active in American Legion Post 101 in Anton Chico.

Mike and Gloria both belong to San Jose Catholic Church in Anton Chico.

Chili Champ:

Figure: Gloria and Mike Stevens the 2014 ICS World Chili Champion and 5-time Champion of the N. M. chili State championship. Courtesy Gloria Stevens.

Mike and Gloria are originally from Chicago. Mike attended the College of Santa Fe and became familiar with N.E. New Mexico and its beauty. Competing in chili competitions also gave Mike and Gloria the calling to retire in Dilia, N.M., therefore becoming the amazing 2014 ICS World Chili Champion and 5-time champion of the N.M. chili state championship. [Gloria Stevens, personal communications, Nov. 13,2022].

Figure: School in Maes.

Amigos de Maes:

The village of Maes is over 30- miles south of Las Vegas. Sparsely populated ranches. Adelino Gallegos's ranchito and the abandoned school have never had electricity or running water.

The school property was donated by the Maestas family. Adelino's ancestors on his grandfather Domingo Maestas family. The village called "Maes" shortened for Maestas.

In a 1953- ¾ ton school bus Adelino Gallegos rode to school. Adelino's primo Adolfo Gallegos was his bus driver. Adelino's bus ride was eight miles one way from Gallegos' home to the school. The daily ride was on a bumpy dirt road.

Grades first to eighth were taught in the little schoolhouse. Some of the teachers for Adelino were Alex Griego, Perfecto Padilla from Trementina, and Tersina Garcia. Adelino graduated from eighth grade. "El colegio" de Adelino.

By the time that Adelino's brother Dolores [Lolo] Gallegos attended school some changes were beginning to take place. Lolo rode on his horse to school and released his horse when he arrived at the little school. The horse immediately headed back to the

Gallegos Ranch. On Monday mornings Lolo was prepared to board with the teacher's family. And by Friday afternoon Lolo was able to go home.

The teacher knew that enrollment was beginning to drop, and the school was possibly going to be consolidated with Las Vegas City Schools. By 1964 the school was consolidated.

Lolo's father Margarito Gallegos began a new job. His job was as a janitor at the city schools. But the janitor job was impossible for him. It was too demanding of a job scraping off gum from floors and cleaning after children was not his ideal job. [Adelino Gallegos, personal communication, Jan. 5, 2020].

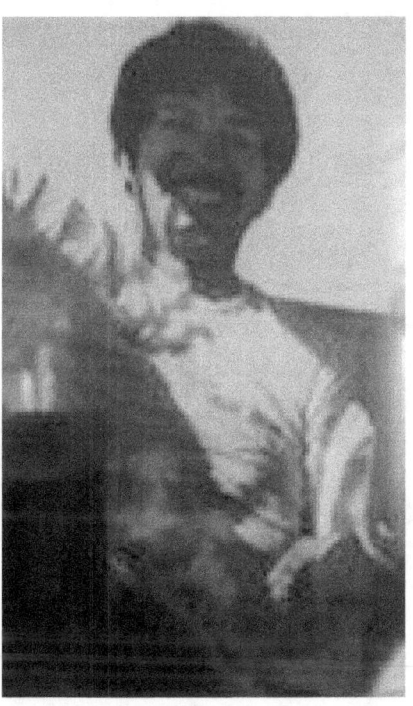

Figure: Dolores {Lolo} Gallegos. Courtesy Adelino Gallegos.

Class of 1953 in Maes:

Figure: Back Row left to right. Manuel Romero [Delfido Romero on Manuel's laps] JJ Jaramillo [bus driver], Benerito Galllegos, David Gallegos, Corrine Maes, Vitalia Medina [prima], Mary Jaramillo. Middle row. Ignacita Barros, Vicenta Baca, Betty Gallegos [prima], Lydia Gonzales, Frida Romero, Ben Baca, Marcelino Segura. Third row. Casimiro Jaramillo, Fermín Maes, Desiderio Baca. Front Row. Adelino Gallegos, Leroy Medina, Debbie Gallegos Salazar, Frances Gallegos. Photo 3/30/1953
Class of 1953 in Maes School. Courtesy of Adelino Gallegos.

Don José Domingo Maestas:

Figure: Jose Domingo Maestas. 1903-1988. Courtesy of Adelino Gallegos.

Domingo's homestead in la Tierra Mala became his home and ranch. A few miles down the road from the Maes old school. The Canadian River and El Sabinoso are close to Vuelta de Loma where Domingo was born.

During the depression, Roosevelt's Work Project Administration provided with the opportunity for Domingo to cut the huge sandstone blocks for the Trementina schoolhouse.

Domingo was a man that took on many challenges of the times. Using the knowledge and working with his hands and his hand tools el martillo de filo [stone-splitting maul] the desbancadora [wide chisel], el punzon [punch], trajadera [a flat] and the martón [sledgehammer]. The tools were simple and required a lot of manpower. Domingo worked on the Corazon Hill Road in San Miguel County laying bed rock.

Domingo's Carvings:

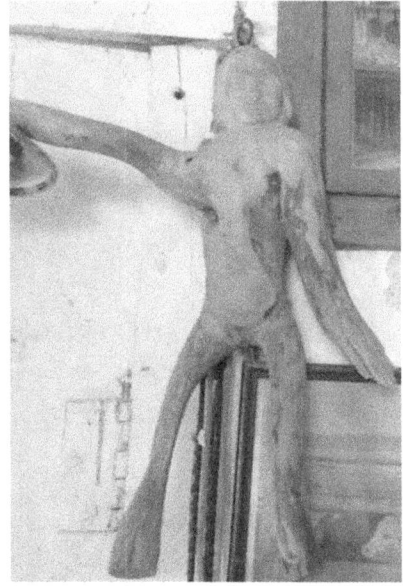 

Figure: Carving. Courtesy Adelino Gallegos. Figure: The Crucifix carving. Courtesy Adelino Gallegos.

Domingo often made observations on wood and roots and was able to visualize and then carve an animal or something beautiful.

Carving into stone and shaping the tombstones along with names and dates as needed became something that he was good at. The headstone was made for family or perhaps barter upon need.

The masonry skill is a European guild that was passed on from stoneworkers imported to Archbishop Lamy. Like the headstones that Augustine Blea created in Harding County. [Robert Brewer, La Herencia, Winter 2008].

Domingo's Museum:

Figure: Domingo Maestas and his Casita the Museum. Courtesy Adelino Gallegos.

Domingo Maestas collected rock objects and many old items that he showcased in his casita museum. He treasured simple things and cared for them. [Adelino Gallegos, personal communication, Jan. 5, 2020].

Figure: Native American Doll.   *Figure: Avocado shaped stone about 16 in. tall. Courtesy Adelino Gallegos.*

Figure: left to right. Carving of root, stone native doll, stone. Courtesy of Adelino Gallegos.

Figure: Padlocks. Courtesy Adelino Gallegos.

Figure: Domingo Maestas Arrowhead collection. Courtesy Adelino Gallegos

Figure: Cowbelles, horse mouth bits. Courtesy Adelino Gallegos.

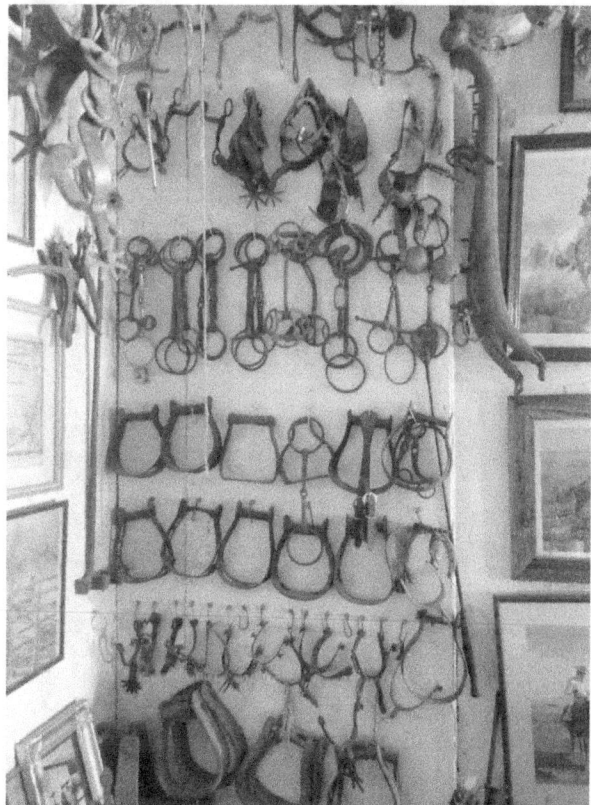

Figure: Collection of Horse mouth bits, spurs, stirrups, wooden lomillo. Courtesy Adelino Gallegos.

Figure: Household Items. Courtesy Adelino Gallegos.

Figure: Carro de bestia [buckboard] Courtesy Adelino Gallegos.

Figure: Sembradora [planter].

Figure: Fragua [forge] used for black smithing. Courtesy Adelino Gallegos.

Figure: Left to Right. Standing Domingo Maestas, Margarito Gallegos. Children on cow left to right. Adelino Gallegos, Lorraine, Eliza. Courtesy Adelino Gallegos.

Wyoming:

Figure: Adelino Gallegos [Lino] Courtesy of Adelino Gallegos.

Adelino attended school "el colegio" in Maes. Finishing eighth grade. By the time he was seventeen years old his father made sure that he got a job. Adelino's father Margarito Gallegos got work in Cokeville, Wyoming en la borrega. Margarito was to look out for 2,000 sheep and Adelino was to be the cook.

Adelino's cooking quarters was the covered wagon. Below the bed is the pantry where storage for flour and food was kept. The suitcases are above his bed where he is sitting.

That first year in 1964 Adelino worked for six months. The following year he worked for seven months. Adelino wondered about getting a better job. La borrega was a hard job and cooking tortillas and frijoles for his dad was not easy. Papá was a picky eater! [Adelino Gallegos, personal communication, Jan. 5, 2020].

Figure: Margarito Gallegos. Courtesy Adelino Gallegos.

Figure: Margarito Gallegos. Mount Vernon. Courtesy Adelino Gallegos.

Calf Tie Down Champion:

Figure: Margarito Gallegos. Courtesy Adelino Gallegos.

  On a calf tie down competition in Maes, Margarito took his caballito Palomino. Margarito's horse was small in stature compared to the competition. Los gringos had tall horses which gave them a reach advantage on the rope.

Margarito had to work a bit harder when throwing a lasso. He did this by stretching his arm to get the extra reach.

Margarito also had a small bottle of corn moonshine in his back pocket. Margarito had a distiller and made his own mula.

The Palomino horse was fast, and Margarito's hind hit the saddle hard during the lasso and busted the bottle of moonshine. But he made his lasso and the calf tied down in 13 seconds. Margarito was the champion! He won $25.00. His wife had some glass to pull off his butt. [Adelino Gallegos, personal communication, Jan. 5, 2020].

Figure: Back Row. Left to Right. Margarito Gallegos, Presides Maestras Gallegos, Eliza Gallegos, Dolores [Lolo] Gallegos, MaryAnn Janet Stillman, George C. Stillman. Front Row. Left to Right. Domingo Maesta, Emiliano Romero, Adelino Gallegos [Groom], Linda M. Stillman Gallegos, Lorraine Gallegos Romero, Simonita Medina, Maestas [1970 wedding]. Courtesy Adelino Gallegos.

Figure: Maes Tornado in 1990. Courtesy Abelino Gallegos.

El Monumento:

Figure: Margarito Gallegos. Monumento [tombstone] made by Margarito Gallegos for himself. Courtesy Adelino Gallegos.

Margarito chose a stone to carve for his own tombstone. He carved "The Sacred Heart of Jesus" into the stone. His granddaughter helped with the monument.

Margarito learned the importance of headstone making from Domingo Maestas, his father-in-law, a trait now becoming a lost legacy. European craftsmen that Archbishop Lamy imported and built the Cathedral in Santa Fe in 1869.

The Depression and Roosevelt's WPA jobs helped communities with building schools. Working with stone gave Domingo the inspiration to use that knowledge on his ranch. Nature inspired his creativity in many ways. [La Herencia, Volume 60 Winter 2008].

BECAUSE NEW MEXICO VOLUNTEERS PROVIDED THE LARGEST CONTINGENT IN COLONEL TEDDY ROOSEVELT's REGIMENT OF ROUGH RIDERS, FOR THE WAR WITH SPAIN IN 1898, 600 OF THE YOUNG VETERANS CAME TO LAS VEGAS FO THEIR FIRST ANNUAL REUNION IN JUNE, 1899 ROOSEVELT WAS GOVERNOR OF NEW YORK AT THAT TIME. AMONG THE HUNDREDS WHO GREETED HIM at the DEPOT AND AT THE HOTEL CASTANEDA WAS A DELEGATION OF PUEBLO INDIANS. (PHOTO COURTESY OF N.M.H.U. ARROTT COLLECTION AND THE PHOTOGRAPHIC SURVEY OF LAS VEGAS).

Source: Clipping. Courtesy Adelino Gallegos.

El Presidente:

Figure: Top Left to Right. Mr. Cavalier, Ms. Cavalier, Kerry Murphy a fire fighter. Front Left to Right Reymundo Maestas, Julian Ray Maestas, 44th President of the United States of America Barack Hussein Obama. Courtesy of Julian Ray Maestas.

Backyard campaign talk given by President Obama at Julian Ray Maestas residence in Albuquerque. This event took place towards the end of President Obama's first term ending in 2012.

Reymundo a life-long Republican was full of excitement to meet President Obama. He respected his President no matter what party he represented. Reymundo said, "no importa que Partido sea, es mi presidente y lo respeto."

Creencias/Querencias:

Hailstorms:

During a hailstorm the believers of creencias will go outside and with a knife cut into the air the sign of the cross. Sprinkling salt and praying for the hail to stop. [Benito Baca, personal communication, July 7, 2021].

Message on Valentine's Day:

Figure: Frances Baca Lucero and Samuel Lucero wedding at Nuestra Señora de Guadalupe en Tecolotito, N. M.

On Feb. 13, Samuel Lucero continuously felt a presence. The presence of Frances, his wife. Although she had been gone for many years. It was about 4:00 in the afternoon. Sam now asked Frances for a message or a sign of some kind to this mysterious feeling. Wanting to know if she was listening.

By midnight Feb. 14, [Valentine's Day] Sam was dreaming of Frances and Violinda [mother] waiting for Juan [dad]. Mother said, "alistense por que hay viene tu dad". Dad had passed away and was now gaining the path to heaven. Sam was asleep at his house in Tecolotito.

It was now 12:00 midnight. Then Sam's cell phone rang at 4-minutes after 12:00. But the phone was turned off and no service was available either. The phone rang about 4 times in a very distinct and special ring. A ring that can't be replicated. Sam got up to check the phone to see who might have called but it was turned off. He went back to bed and felt chills. While dozing off again the phone rang again 5- or 10- minute rings from Heaven. Samuel felt chills the second time again. Yes, Frances had communicated Dad's passage to Heaven. [Samuel Lucero, personal communication, August 25, 2018].

Clines Corner's:

Margie, a teenager, was working at the cafeteria in Clines Corners. Two other girls worked with her. The restaurant is close to the interstate. And a snowstorm was accumulating lots of snow. Many kinds of people come into the cafeteria for food.

A man walked inside that day and asked for food. He was hungry and had no money the man was wearing a robe and had long hair.

The two girls refused to feed him because they weren't allowed to give out food. That could cause them to lose their jobs. But Margie decided to help the man even if it meant losing her job. The man blessed Margie. The girls said, "you're going to lose your job!"

Margie told the man, "Get from the cafeteria whatever you want to eat." He chose to eat only bread and milk and then thanked Margie. Then he sat and ate.

He told Margie something very strange. He said, "there are three keys in life." The first key is "love". The second key is to "honor" the father and mother. The third key is "trust and believe". He walked outside marking his footprints on the snow. But suddenly turned the corner and he was gone, he had vanished. [Margie Lucero Chavez, personal communication, Sept., 30, 2018].

Jerry Salas:

Figure: Jerry Salas. Courtesy Isabel Salas Barela, Lorraine Barela Pohl.

Dichos:

Como es el Dicho:

1. "Alcen sus camas porque si se pasan de las doce se mete el diablo". By José Encinias [Coco]
2. "Le dijo una oreja al otra. Que extraño vivemos en el mismo bloque y nunca nos hemos visto". By José Encinias [Coco]
3. "Que fuera de nosotros los feos y si no hubiera malos gustos".
4. "Al haber gatos ni ratones quedan".
5. "El que tiene tienda que la atienda si no que la venda". By Juan Lucero Jr.
6. "Ave María Purísima". By Eulalia Leyba Lucero
7. "Vale más ir a clavar el hacha donde la clava en papa". By Benny Gonzales [Juga]
8. "Al trabajo y a los chingazos muy pocos le entran". By Juan Tenorio
9. "Dios dijo que has tu inteligencia que yo te ayudare". By María Otero
10. "Se anda curando en salud". By Violinda Castillo Lucero
11. "Están cortadas con la misma tijera". By Pacomio Ortega
12. "Valió madre la sobada". By Reymundo Maestas
13. "Ya se nos hizo gorda Antonia". By Joe Encinias [Coco]
14. "Esa es tos de camposanto". By Ramon Lucero
15. "El que hambre tiene en frijoles piensa". By Juan Tenorio
16. "Esa risa se va a volver llanto". By Violinda Castillo Lucero
17. "Siempre está más verde en el otro lado del cerco".

18. "Donde quiera andas metiendo tus narices". By Luisa Lucero Tenorio

19. "No está bien encabado". By Reymundo Maestas

20. "Dejaron al ratón cuidando el queso". By Reymundo Maestas

21. "Cuanto a de volar". By Felipe Tenorio

22. "Donde quiera se cuecen habas".

23. "Es de mala medra". By Arturo Lucero

24. "Es muy malas tripas". By Ramon Lucero

25. "Es un verdugo para trabajar". By Telesfor Lucero

26. "Tienen más grandes los ojos que la pansa". By Eulalia Leyba Lucero

27. "Bueno", "Hasta la otra tresquila". By Andalecio Romero

28. "Ya el cuero está en el agua". By Juan Lucero Jr.

29. "Andan colgando jeta". By Eulalia Leyba Lucero

30. "Se nos pintó un venado". By Esteban Romero [Sticker]

31. "Que pasen días y vengan pesos". By Bentura Maestas

32. "Ya mero la vez un pobre". By David Lucero Sr.

33. "Esta como un reloj de peso". By Miguel Gonzales

34. "No les des mucho cabresto".

35. "Le voy a pegar donde duele más". By Leroy Sandoval

36. "Ese tiene más vueltas que un tornillo". By Manuel Lucero

37. "Y luego viene el chancludo".

38. "Y luego viene el penco".

39. "No pueden ver ojos en otra cara". By Prudencio Villanueva

40. "Yo no le escondo la vela a nadie". By Eulalia Leyba Lucero

41. "Se andan chacoteando".

42. "Quien está pelando este pollo"? By Lugie Romo

43. "Se pagan las que se deben".

44. "Está bien camalteado".

45. "El que no llora no mama". By Sandoval

46. "Estas cagado y no te oles". By Benito Baca

47. "Está muy corrido sin aceite".

48. "La visita y los muertos a los tres días hieden". By Reymundo Maestas

49. "Mas carne para los leones". By Cecilio Villanueva

50. "Ya se lo llevo el demoño".

51. "Aquí pelando ojos". By Freddie Lucero

52. "Esos se van a morir con un ratón en la boca". By Eulalia Leyba Lucero

53. "No toquen esas armas por que se mete el diablo". By Eulalia Leyba Lucero

54. "Se fue con la cola entre las piernas". By Leroy Sandoval

55. "Donde quiera anda metiendo la cola".

56. "Andamos con las medias caídas".

57. "Están como las de Sonora". By Benerito Lucero

58. "Te voy a dar hasta que mi corazón descanse".

59. "La verdad la cuestión". By Dionicio Castillo

60. "Si lo agarro le voy a dar hasta por debajo la lengua".

61. "Ay viene haciéndose el mansito".

62. "Quizás piensa que estoy cagando dinero".

63. "No es más lepero porque no es más grande". By José Tenorio

64. "Se le caen las alas a uno".

65. "Anda largo y tendido".

66. "Haciendo chile con la cola". By Reymundo Maestas

67. "Le prestas un dedo y agarran toda la mano". By José Encinias [Coco]

68. "Este es gato de casa". By Andalecio Romero

69. "Se ahondo la carrera". By Juan Tenorio

70. "El que asiste perro ajeno pierde el pan y pierde el perro".

71. "El mejor hombre merece que lo quemen con leña verde".

72. "Es un pintito para tirar piedras". By Vicente Armijo

73. "Lo barato cuesta caro".

74. "Ya pintaron vereda".

75. "Ya se volvió boruca".

76. "Ya le anda buscando pies al gato". By Ramon Lucero

77. "Los chingazos quitan lo burro".

78. "Se hace las muelas de gallo". By Arturo Lucero

79. "Se peleo con el peine esta mañana".

80. "Lo pesque con la mano en la masa". By José Encinias [Coco]

81. "Le quedo la manita duce [dulce]". By Don Felipe Tenorio

82. "Andan pescando brujas; cuando andan con la camisa al revés".

83. "Se le hincho la cabeza". By José Tenorio

84. "Ay viene haciéndose el tontito para chingar con las dos manos". By Betty Olguin

85. "Cada chango en su columpio". By José Lucero

86. "Este tiene el ojo más grande que la pansa". By Eulalia Leyba Lucero

87. "Se me hace que te están chingando con el mandado". By Betty Olguin

88. "Donde fuerza ay ni coraje da". By Reymundo Maestas

89. "Salimos rayando el sol". By Don Felipe Tenorio

90. "Ya cage el palo". By Rubel Lucero

91. "Nos rayó el disco". By Gilbert Tenorio

92. "Ya cagaron la bolera". By Don Melaquias

93. "Ya andan con que la puse y no el hayo". By Don Melaquias Tenorio

94. "A buen santo te recomiendas".

95. "Se pinto un venado". By Andalecio Romero

96. "Ese es más resbaloso como una trucha". By Horacio Olguin

97. "Para Rivera un baile". By Benerito Lucero

98. "Ya me parraron el macho". By Henry Padilla

99. "Sabe de qué pata cojella".

100. "No miras la viga que traes en el ojo y tanto que te espantas". By Benito Baca

101. "A ese lo van a quemar con leña verde". By Violinda Castillo Lucero

102. "Haber cómo le va cuando se ahonda la carrera". By

103. "Entre baranda y bola". By Rosa Montaño

104. "Para morir uno, no necesitas más que estar vivo". By Juan Tenorio

105. "El que sale a bailar pierde su lugar".

106. "Cada cabeza es un mundo". By Violinda Castillo Lucero.

107. "No es araña que sube a media pared".

108. "Ay te pones al dime te diré".

109. "Para hechar mentiras y comer pescado debes tener cuidado". By Reymundo Maestas

110. "Casa de herrero cuchara de palo".

111. "Pon te truchas".

112. "Le busca pies al gato". By Juan Tenorio

113. "Una punta para los preguntones". Don Melaquias Tenorio

114. "Con lo que no cuesta se hace fiesta".

115. "No más el sol calienta dioquis".

116. "Lo fino entra por la boca". By juan Lucero Jr.

117. "La gente habla más de lo que más les hace falta". By Pacomio Ortega

118. "Donde ay fuerza ni coraje da". By Nick Hern

119. "Ya viene amolándose las uñas." By Eulalia Leyba Lucero

120. "Todas las mujeres están cortadas con la misma tijera".

"Dios tarda, pero no olvida". By Don Felipe Tenorio

Figure: Nelson's Mercantile. Anton Chico, N.M.

Acknowledgments

Thanks to my husband for the patience and encouragement in pursuing the writing of a second book.

Thanks to my son Leroy C. Tenorio for all his time and assistance in editing, formatting, and designing the book cover.

Thanks to all the people, family, friends, and many cousins that have roots and hold Anton Chico Dear to their Hearts and happy to tell their story.

Bibliography

Ancestry Military, Registration Card Zacarias Salas.

Carlsbad Project Water Operations and Water Supply Conservation FEIS.

Cook, Mary J. Straw. Doña Tules. The University of New Mexico Press, Albuquerque, 2007.

Find my past transcript U.S. Census 1920.

Fourth Judicial District of the Territory of New Mexico, County of San Miguel. "Juan Marquez et al., vs Agapito Sandoval et al., Civil Docket 4149 p.p. 112, 126.

Gallegos, Jose. Guadalupe org. Wikipedia.

Garcia, Francisco. Ancestry 'War Records Library Museum of N.M., Historical Society of N.M.".

Hispanic Genealogical Research Center of New Mexico, Baptisms San Miguel del Vado Pecos Mission 1799-1829, p.52.

Hispanic Genealogical Research Center of New Mexico Marriages, Anton Chico La Yglesia de San Jose April 1857- December 1940 p. 26.

Hispanic Genealogical Research Center of New Mexico José Rumaldo Lucero + María Lucia Gonzales.

Libro de Partidos de Casamientos, La Iglesia de Anton Chico 1857 to 1940].

Marriage License County of San Miguel, State of New Mexico, Dionicio Castillo and Miquelita Tapia.

Nostrand L. Richard. El Cerrito, New Mexico, 2003, p.186.

Saint Joseph's Catholic Church, Anton Chico, New Mexico, baptismal and marriage records.

www.colonias nm.com/html

www.hgrcnm.org/webtrees/compact.

www.hgrcnm.orgwebtrees/individual

Sacramental Records from the Archives of the Archdiocese of Santa Fe, N. Mex. Baptisms Antón Chico La Yglesia de San José 1857-1897.

Sacramental Records from the Archives of the Archdiocese of Santa Fe, N. Mex. Marriages Antón Chico La Yglesia de San José April 1857-December 1940.

Salas, Placido. Compact tree, Hispanic Genealogy Center of New Mexico

Salas, Zacarias. Ancestry Records of Military Service.

Sisneros, Severiano R. Jr., A Brief History of The Anton Chico Land Grant From Its Beginning Until The Present.

Special Schedule San Miguel County New Mexico Territory Eleventh Census of the U.S.

Stanley, F., The Antón Chico Story (New Mexico) Story: 1975.

U.S. Federal Census Transcriptions. 1910, 1930, Guadalupe County Territory and State of New Mexico.

U.S. Federal Census. 1900, La Pintada, Guadalupe, State of New Mexico.

U.S. Federal Census. Transcriptions. 1860, 1880, 1900, 1910, San Miguel County Territory and State of New Mexico.

U.S. Federal Census. Transcriptions. 1900, San Miguel County Territory, La Liendre and State of New Mexico.

U.S. Federal Census. Transcriptions. 1880, Santa Fe County Territory, Galisteo and State of New Mexico.

Yolanda Lucero Tenorio daughter of Juan Lucero Jr. and Violinda Castillo Lucero. Yolanda was born in Tecolotito, New Mexico at the home of her maternal grandfather, Dionicio Castillo. She is the oldest of eight children. She resides In Tecolotito with her family.

Earning a BA and MA degree from New Mexico Highlands University. She taught her first year in Santa Rosa Elementary and retired from the Anton Chico Schools.

She is not a writer by profession but has chosen to document stories about the ways of life for family, community members, and for our children.

Having farmed and ranched has given her the opportunity to listen to the elders and members of the community. "Last of the Dons" was written in 2018 but many stories remained to be documented in hopes of preserving them.

www.ingramcontent.com/pod-product-compliance
Lightning Source LLC
Chambersburg PA
CBHW081144230426
43664CB00018B/2798